Speak Up, Speak Out

Women *at* Work

Inspiring conversations, advancing together

The **HBR WOMEN AT WORK SERIES** spotlights the real challenges and opportunities women experience throughout their careers. With interviews from the popular podcast of the same name and related articles, stories, and research, these books provide inspiration and advice for taking on issues at work such as inequity, advancement, and building community. Featuring detailed discussion guides, this series will help you spark important conversations about where we're at and how to move forward.

Books in the series include:

Making Real Connections

Speak Up, Speak Out

You, the Leader

Women *at* Work
Inspiring conversations, advancing together

Speak Up, Speak Out

Harvard Business Review Press
Boston, Massachusetts

Printed in the United States of America

10 9 8 7 6 5 4 3 2 1

Cataloging-in-Publication data is forthcoming.

ISBN: 978-1-64782-222-4
eISBN: 978-1-64782-223-1

The paper used in this publication meets the requirements of the American National Standard for Permanence of Paper for Publications and Documents in Libraries and Archives Z39.48-1992

CONTENTS

SECTION TWO

Speak Out on Sexual Harassment

SECTION THREE

Speak Out Against Racism

SECTION FOUR

Men

Be Allies and Amplify Voices

INTRODUCTION

Get Ready to Speak Up

by Amanda Kersey, producer of *Women at Work*

I rarely said anything during the morning meeting in my first full-time job as a production assistant in a newsroom. I had ideas, no doubt. But I was shy and intimidated not only by the sheer number of people crowded together in that conference room but also by how many of them were quick to interrupt, put down, or just tune out anyone they didn't care to hear from. The threat of ridicule kept me quiet—and frustrated. I'd majored in journalism hoping to start somewhere like this. Editors in this room had *hired me* to be here. And now that I was, why couldn't I get the words out?

Looking back, I cut myself slack for not speaking up much: A lot of us struggle. It's not only because there's a learning curve to being able to break into a discussion and say what you came to say while deflecting interrupters.

(I remember longing to raise my hand or praying someone would call on me.) It's also that working on a team means encountering stifling biases, like old-fashioned, lingering expectations that women be agreeable and passive. Handling incivility and other barriers to a healthy exchange of ideas requires knowledge and practice.

Helping readers and listeners leverage their voices to better their careers and workplaces has been a goal of *Women at Work* from the beginning. Our debut podcast episode focused on communication, and since then we've covered various aspects of speaking up including the art of claiming credit, strategic self-disclosure, how to maneuver around double standards when announcing a decision you've made, how to press a boss for useful feedback. Knowing how to speak up against individuals and systems that try to silence women is just as critical, which is why we also cover, on the podcast and in this book, tactics for confronting sexual harassment and racism.

Improvising an appropriate response to harassment and hate is difficult. If you're the target, the emotional shock can make responding inconceivable. If you're the witness, the misconduct can leave you speechless, especially if you've never prepared for work to go so far south. The strategies, sample language, and leadership skills detailed in this collection give you options for dealing with uncomfortable scenarios before you're in them.

After several years of working at HBR and producing *Women at Work*, I marvel at how I'm now usually able to express what in the past I would have held inside. I don't just contribute to meetings; I run them. I give presentations. I moderate live events. How did I get here? In part, by following what I've learned from the show about speaking up, such as Amy B's advice for getting over ourselves: "It's not about you; it's about the idea. And when you get to that point, you liberate yourself from all those doubts . . . and you make it so much easier to get your ideas across." That perspective helped me release some self-doubt, and I spoke more fluidly—just as she said I would.

But more than any tactic I've tried, trusting that my colleagues genuinely wanted to hear from me made me feel safe to put myself out there. I have a boss and other leaders in my corner who listen, who've made civility on their team the norm, who ask for my perspective in public, and who give me opportunities to test my ever-expanding comfort zone. If you're a leader, how you speak and listen to your employees has a great influence on whether or not they're contributing to their full potential. The insight and advice in this book will show you how to use whatever power you have to elevate your voice and the voices of the women you work with. Finally, the questions within the discussion guide at the end of the book will help you reflect or facilitate conversations among colleagues and friends.

Speaking up and speaking out are skills you will need throughout your career. Anticipating challenges ranging from those who talk over you to harassment allows you to prepare what you'll do and say and gives you time to build relationships with allies. You can strengthen your voice. You can be heard.

SECTION ONE

Speak Up

You Deserve to Be Heard

1

Make Yourself Heard

A conversation with Deborah Tannen

Have you ever been in a meeting and shared an idea, only to have it ignored? Then, 10 minutes later, a guy shares the same idea, and your boss says, "Great idea!" Or maybe you've been told you apologize too much, don't speak up enough, or that you need more "confidence" or "leadership presence."

So much of how women lead comes back to how we speak. Amy Bernstein, Sarah Green Carmichael, and Nicole Torres spoke with Deborah Tannen, a Georgetown University linguistics professor and author of the bestsellers *You Just Don't Understand: Women and Men in Conversation* and *Talking from 9 to 5: Women and Men at Work*, about how and why women's speech patterns differ from men's and the effects of these differences.

In the 1990s more women were in the office, increasingly working alongside men or above them, not for them. Deborah Tannen was concerned about these women being heard and respected by their male colleagues. In her 1995 workplace training video, *Talking 9 to 5*, Tannen shared an anecdote that is still painfully relatable today, three decades later. *Have you ever said something at a meeting and had it ignored? Then someone else said the same thing and it was picked up as a great idea—his great idea? Have you ever told someone to do something, and then it wasn't done? Or it was done wrong?*

NICOLE TORRES: What does your research tell you about how gendered conversational patterns at work can put women at a disadvantage?

DEBORAH TANNEN: A ritual that men often use, which women can take literally, is ritual opposition. Just as little boys often spend time play fighting with their friends much more than little girls do, as adults, men often use an oppositional stance to get things done.

SARAH GREEN CARMICHAEL: For example, rather than supporting somebody else's idea, they'll try to point out the weaknesses; they'll challenge it as a way of helping somebody explore the idea.

AMY BERNSTEIN: And that makes me run away.

NICOLE: You wrote about the power of talk for HBR in 1995. What, if anything, has changed about how women are speaking and being heard in the workplace.

DEBORAH: My impression is that not much has changed. I have been giving talks to various organizations pretty much nonstop since then. And I get the same response: "That's exactly what's happening to me." "I experienced that just yesterday." "You've just told the story of my life."

NICOLE: If women are still struggling to be heard for the same reasons today, what's driving that?

DEBORAH: I trace the way women and men *tend* to speak at work to the ways children learn to use language growing up. Of course, nothing is true of all women or all men. We have many other influences on our style than our gender. But there are tendencies that girls and boys learn as kids playing in same-sex groups. Girls tend to talk in ways that downplay their authority. If they talk in ways that play up the fact that they are the leader in the group or that they think they're good at something, the other girls will criticize them: "She's bossy." "She thinks she's something." "She's stuck up." Compare that with the way boys tend to maintain their position in the group. They talk up what they're good at, maybe even make it a game where they're trying to top each other. The leader of the group is someone who tells the other boys what to do and gets it to stick. If we move into the workplace, a person in authority has to tell others what to do. Frequently, women find ways to do it that doesn't seem too bossy and downplays their authority.

A college president told me of this experience. She had said to her assistant, "Could you do me a favor?" before asking her to do something. A member of the board who happened to overhear took her aside and said, "Don't forget, you're the president." Her opening, "Could you do me a favor?" sounded to him as if she thought she didn't have the authority to ask her own assistant to do something. In fact, she knew the assistant had to do whatever she asked, so she was saving face for the assistant by asking it in a way that was, in her view, simply polite. She didn't mean that literally.

SARAH: I have noticed that women try to make requests and all kinds of leadership maneuvers less direct by phrasing things as questions. For example, a woman in a meeting says, "I'm not quite sure I'm following. Can someone recap for me?" if they think that the person running the meeting should have done that but didn't in the beginning. Or, "Can someone please explain what the Q3 results mean?" Even if they themselves know, but they think someone else in the group needs that information.

DEBORAH: That's a great example of how women will often talk in ways that save face for other people. And it's interpreted as something internal about them. In these cases, others might see them as less competent because they ask for the recap or the information.

NICOLE: This was a really interesting take on confidence. The narrative is usually that women are socialized to be less confident. But it seems like you're saying they're actually socialized to *sound* less confident.

DEBORAH: Yes, absolutely. Laurie Heatherington and her colleagues did a study where they asked hundreds of incoming college students to predict the grades that they were going to get in their first year. There were two conditions. Half of them were asked to do it in a public way, either orally to the interviewer or by writing it on a piece of paper that the interviewer immediately read. The other was private. Write what you expect and seal it in an envelope without your name. The findings were fascinating. When the expectations were public, women predicted much lower grades for themselves than men did. When they were private, the grades predicted were the same for the women and the men. So, the women who predicted their grades publicly were downplaying what they really expected so they wouldn't come across as too full of themselves.

AMY: There might be something different going on with credit taking and women. For some of us, taking credit is kind of repugnant. Have you seen anything on that front?

DEBORAH: Yes. I observed that women frequently said "we" when talking about something they personally had done or accomplished. I also observed men saying "I" about things that they were not individually, personally, responsible for. That has a lot to do with our sense of what's appropriate. Many women feel it's boastful to say "I." They avoid the word "I." So, they'll say "we" to be gracious about the people that they work with but assume other people will know that they really did it. That's similar to this more general pattern that many women felt: "If I do a good job, it will be noticed. I don't have to call attention to what I've done." Many men realize that they should call attention to what they've done or people won't know. Women have taken for granted or assume these ways of speaking are appropriate and realistic. The phenomenon I often refer to is the double bind. A double bind is a situation where you have two sets of requirements, but anything you do to fulfill one set actually violates the other. We have expectations for how women should speak, such as being self-deprecating and sounding tentative, and we have expectations for how a person in authority should speak, such as being self-assured and sounding certain. If women speak as women are expected to, they are underestimated. If they speak as a person in authority is expected to, they are seen as too aggressive and people don't like them. Men may not meet expectations, but they don't face a double bind because expectations for how men should speak are similar to expectations for a person in authority. It's a challenge for women to find some middle ground.

AMY: What does it sound like to successfully navigate that?

DEBORAH: I'll give an example. A woman has to tell a subordinate to do something. If she says something like, "Do you think you could do this by 4?" The high pitch, the rising intonation, all of that would be polite and not too imposing. People would like her but might see her as lacking authority. She could say, "Do this by 4." That would be authoritative but might come across as too assertive for a woman. She could say something like, "I need this by 4. Do you think you could do that?" So, it's something in between the very self-effacing and the very declarative.

SARAH: Some of the conversational rituals, as you call them, that women tend to use are really interesting, such as apologizing when something's not their fault but just because something bad happened. In that case, you point out, it means "I'm sorry that happened." It's not an apology, but it is often heard as one. Or ritualistically complimenting other people, especially other women.

DEBORAH: Sometimes conversational rituals backfire when the other person doesn't do their part. Women are often told they apologize too much. Sometimes a woman will use an apology to get the other person to apologize. Let's say there was a meeting; you're a woman and the boss. A subordinate didn't come to the meeting, although he was supposed to. You might say something like, "Gee, sorry you weren't at the meeting. If I forgot to tell you about it, I'm sorry. It was really pretty important." You know you told him about the meeting. You have apologized for A; he is supposed to apologize for B. So, he should say, and you would expect him to say, "Oh, yeah, you did tell me. I'm sorry; something came up and I couldn't make it, but I'll make sure to find out what went on and it won't happen again." If he says, "Yeah, make sure you tell me next time," it's almost like sitting on a seesaw. You sit on your side and you trust the other person to sit on their side. If they get off, you plop to the ground and wonder how you got there. *What did I do?* But it really wasn't anything you did. It's that the other person did not do their part of the conversational ritual.

NICOLE: If conversational rituals have changed because there are more women in the workplace and more female leaders, you'd think they would introduce their own conversational rituals and there would be more complimenting, more apologizing, and more recognition that "I'm sorry" may mean "I'm sorry that happened." Why aren't those behaviors and rituals more valued now if they're more common?

DEBORAH: When I did this research back in the early '90s, I was quite convinced that when there were more women in the workplace, the standards would change. So, in a way, I'm disappointed and also surprised that they haven't. The explanation I would surmise is that a sense of how a person in authority should speak or behave is still based on an image of a man in authority. We still associate authority with men.

NICOLE: After Deborah left, Amy, Sarah, and I chatted about how we talk at the office as three women working as editors at HBR.

SARAH: I have found it really hard to reach a happy medium between backing off some behaviors, like apologizing, that I know are undermining me and also finding a more assertive way to speak that doesn't sound too strong.

AMY: Put yourself in the listener's position. It is such a bore to listen to someone apologize and the endless on-ramps to the point. Just stop it. You're not doing anyone any favors, particularly yourself. But the people listening to you just want to hear what you're trying to say. They don't want to hear all the atmospherics around it. The other piece of advice I'll give, and you didn't ask for it, is to get over yourself. It's not about you. It's about the idea. When you get to that point, you liberate yourself from all those doubts and all the communication of those doubts. You make it so much easier to get your ideas across and become so much more interesting.

SARAH: Earlier in my career, I had attempted to cut out a lot of these conversational female tics. The advice I got from someone who had my best interests at heart was, "Sarah, when you talk, you're not deferential enough. Instead of just blurting out your idea, you need to say, 'Well, this is just one idea, but . . . ,' or 'I could be wrong, but . . .'" And I was really taken aback by that. I actually told the senior male who was giving me this advice, "Oh, it's funny you noticed that, because I had made a conscious effort to stop doing that because I had heard it is something young women do that undermines them."

AMY: That makes me absolutely crazy hearing that. That is such bad advice. It may have been well intentioned and may have been delivered with love. But to tell a young woman to be more deferential is so undermining. An exceptionally bright and articulate young woman does have a steeper hill to climb. There's no question about that. But a good manager helps her climb it without stepping on every little landmine. And it is a mine field out there—we all know that.

Adapted from "Make Yourself Heard," Women at Work *podcast, season 1, episode 1, January 24, 2018.*

2

How to Handle Interrupting Colleagues

by Francesca Gino

You're giving a presentation on the company's strategic direction when one of your colleagues interrupts you. You pause, address his question, and continue with your point—until he interrupts again. Sound familiar?

All of us have known colleagues, friends, or romantic partners who seem unable to let us finish a sentence. How do you handle them effectively? There are a number of tactics. But it is important to understand when and why people interrupt others.

When and Why People Interrupt Others

Here are some of the aspects to consider about what may be driving people to interrupt others.

Different cultural norms

At the beginning of my relationship with my husband, I constantly interrupted him. Knowing that I love arguments based on data and good evidence, he showed up for one of our dates with a research paper titled "Overlapping Talk and the Organization of Turn-Taking for Conversation." The first sentence reads, "The orderly distribution of opportunities to participate in social interaction is one of the most fundamental preconditions for viable social organization." I got his point.

After that, I started watching out for my tendency to interrupt, which I blamed on my being Italian. (Italians are often expressive and verbal, and we tend to take interruptions as a sign of interest in the conversation rather than a lack of interest in what someone is saying.) Later, I even found some empirical support for the idea that culture plays a role in interruptions when reading about how people from individualistic and collectivistic cultures interact in conversation.[1]

In one study, Japanese participants (whose culture is collectivistic) tended to switch their usual cooperative interruption style (interruptions asking for clarifications) to the more intrusive North American style when they were engaged in conversations in English with Americans.[2] In addition, the number of intrusive interruptions was higher in conversations between Japanese and American participants conducted in English than in conversations between two Japanese participants in Japanese. Similarly, in other studies with different cultures, the person speaking a second language often switched to the speech style of the native speaker.

Because of my own tendency to interrupt, I was curious to learn more about interruptions and what predicts dominance during conversations and meetings.

Status

From the literature, I learned that heritage is not the only factor that affects interruption. Studies of group discussions and conversations during meetings have found that status is another.[3] High-status people are asked their opinions more often, talk more, receive more positive comments, are chosen as leaders more frequently, are more likely to influence their group's decisions, and in general dominate the conversation. Studies of conversations involving couples and families have also found such status effects.

People tend to dominate conversations and interrupt when they feel more powerful than others in the room or when they want to signal power to others. In my research with Leigh Tost of the University of Southern California and Rick Larrick of Duke University, we found that when we induced people to feel powerful, by having them write about a time they had power over other people, they gave more weight to their own opinions than to a more informed adviser's when making decisions.[4] In another study, team leaders who were induced to feel powerful did most of the talking during the team discussion and interrupted frequently.[5] As a result, these leaders failed to learn about critical information that other team members had.

In my executive education classes, I find that students who are randomly assigned to the role of team leader experience a sense of power and overconfidence that leads them to dominate the team's conversation. They talk more, interrupt, give directives—and listen very little. Consequently, they fail to learn from others, with detrimental consequences for team performance.

How to Handle Interrupters

Now that you've considered what may be driving the person to interrupt, how should you deal with them? You could give them academic research showing them the error of their ways, as my husband did while we were dating. But I would argue that the following simple strategies are more successful.

Preempt the interrupter

Of course you can ask the person who interrupted to allow you to finish what you were saying. Even better, before you start talking, preview what you plan to say and stipulate when it's OK to break in. Workplace consultant Laura Rose suggests saying something like, "There are a lot of different pieces to this explanation, so please bear with me. I want to tell you the entire story. Then I want us to wrap around and get your thoughts on specific details." This type of preview may stop the interrupter before they start.

Hold a constructive private conversation

If the interruptions continue, speak to the person in private. Give the interrupter the benefit of the doubt; they may not realize their tendency to interrupt (as was the case with me). Talk to the person about what you've observed and for how long, and explain how it affects you (and others, if appropriate). This straight talk, when framed constructively, is more likely to produce a behavioral change. (See the sidebar "How to Confront an Interrupter.")

How to Confront an Interrupter

BY AMY GALLO

To make the task of confronting colleagues seem less awkward and intimidating, we brought in our in-house expert on difficult conversations, Amy Gallo.

Whether you're interrupted once in a while or dealing with a chronic interrupter, here are some things to keep in mind to set you up for a productive interaction.

- **Speak up in the moment.** When you're interrupted in the flow of the conversation, say something like: "I have something to contribute here. Would it be OK if I got through to the end of my point before I took questions? I have a hard time finishing my thought when I'm interrupted. But I'm happy to hear your thoughts as soon as I finish. I'll let you know when I'm done."

- **Approach chronic interrupters privately.** If interruptions are a persistent problem, approach the interrupter for a one-on-one conversation, not in the heat of the moment. Go into that conversation saying, "Can I talk to you about something?" It's good to start a difficult conversation with a question. "Hey, I'm about to say something; are you ready?" helps them give you a little bit of permission. They're consenting to the conversation.

- **Don't assign negative intentions.** When you have the conversation with the interrupter, frame your observation as neutrally as possible: "You may not realize what's happening in the meetings, but I feel like I'm being interrupted multiple times. And I don't know what I'm doing to contribute to the problem, but I'd love to talk with you about how we can change our dynamic in the meeting." That puts you both on the same side of the table. You're not leveling accusations; you're not being antagonistic. But you're saying, "We have a problem; here's what I perceive it to be. Can we talk about it together?"
- **Give specific examples.** Some people don't even realize what they're doing, so it can be useful to share examples. You can say something like, "When I was talking about the strategy for this new project and I was laying out my thoughts, you interrupted me multiple times. I know you were eager to get your opinions heard, but it would have been helpful if you waited until I was done to do that." You don't want it to sound like an email that you would send to HR. You want to strike the tone of a collaborative discussion in which you're solving a problem you have—together.

Excerpted from "Make Yourself Heard," *Women at Work* podcast, season 1, episode 1, January 24, 2018.

Enlist the group

If you'd prefer to avoid embarrassing the interrupter, you can address the whole group without pointing fingers. Ask the group to reflect on whether you are communicating effectively together and what could be improved. This strategy would allow every member, including you, to raise their awareness of challenges facing the group, a first important step in addressing problems like this one.

By addressing past interruptions, you'll be able to avoid future ones and encourage more balanced, effective conversations.

Adapted from content posted on hbr.org, February 22, 2017 (product #H03HEP).

3

You Don't Just Need One Leadership Voice—You Need Many

by Amy Jen Su

We often equate developing a leadership voice with finding ways to appear more confident. We assume that our success depends upon mimicking someone else, increasing our self-promotion, or saying things louder than others. But rather than living with impostor syndrome or feeling exhausted by wearing your game face all day, you can build a truer confidence by more intentionally focusing on cultivating many different parts of your leadership voice each day. Ultimately, you should cultivate enough parts of your voice so that no matter the leadership situation or audience you find yourself facing, you can respond in an authentic, constructive, and effective way. So, what are the various voices to access within yourself and cultivate over time? And what are the situations that warrant each voice?

Your voice of character

First and foremost, consider the voice of your character. This is the part of your voice that is constant and consistent. It is grounded in fundamental principles about whom you choose to be and what guides and motivates your interactions with others. I've had leaders share that they hold key leadership principles in mind such as "Give the benefit of the doubt," "Don't take things personally," "Focus on what's best for the business," or "Be direct with respect" when walking into a difficult conversation, meeting, or potential conflict. Anchoring ourselves in the character we know we have keeps us from becoming chameleons, acting out of a fight-or-flight reaction, or only showing respect when there is a commercial gain or benefit—while being uncivil to others who we believe hold less value. A voice of character is ultimately about who you are and the intentions and motivations that guide your speech and actions.

Your voice of context

As you take on increasingly senior roles, your view and perspective of the business grow. You hold more of the big picture. Part of the job then becomes finding ways to express and communicate that bigger picture to others. Too often, in the race against time, we dive right into the details of a presentation, meeting, or conversation, without taking an extra few minutes to appropriately set the stage and share critical context. Places where you can bring more of your voice of context include:

- Sharing vision, strategy, or upcoming organizational change with others
- Presenting to executives, and being clear on what you are there for and what you need
- Kicking off a meeting with your team and giving the bigger picture for the topic at hand
- Making your decision-making criteria or rationale transparent to others

Your voice of clarity

In a world of high-intensity workplaces, you have the opportunity to be the voice of clarity and help your team stay focused on the most-important priorities. Leaders who envision new possibilities, muse out loud, or have knee-jerk reactions run the risk of teams trying to deliver on their every whim; these teams end up scattered, spread thin, and unfocused, falling short on delivering on the most-important wins. Here are a few ways you can be the voice of clarity to help channel others’ energies more productively:

- At the start of the year, sit down with each direct report to prioritize and clarify what the big wins are in each of their areas. One client of mine shared how she asks each team member: "If we were to publish this in a newspaper, what would you want the big headlines to be for you and your team at the end of the year?"

- Periodically come back to helping your direct reports reprioritize what's on their plates. You can do this in one-on-one meetings or with your entire team.
- Empower your team to say no.

Your voice of curiosity

As a leader, you have a responsibility to give direction, share information, and make important decisions. But you shouldn't approach every situation as if you have all the answers or as if you need to advise on, problem-solve, or fix everything in front of you. In many cases, being the voice of curiosity is a better choice for the situation. As one of my clients once shared about facing pushback from others, "While I'm confident in my own business judgment and instincts, I know that my organization has hired really smart people. Therefore, if one of my peers or team members has a different perspective or pushes back, I don't take it personally. I get really curious to understand where they are coming from first so that we can get to the best solution." Some situations where bringing your voice of curiosity can help you and your colleagues move forward:

- When you're engaging in work that is interdependent, and a better solution will come from hearing all perspectives in the room before coming to a final decision
- When you're coaching a direct report, asking good questions to help them grow in new ways, explore issues they're facing, or support their career development
- When you're in a difficult conversation where hearing out the other person is an important part of diffusing emotion, understanding each party's needs and views, and then figuring out the best way forward

Your voice of connection

As your span of control or influence grows, it can become increasingly more difficult to make a connection with a broadening set of colleagues, strategic networks, and teams. We often have folks working for us many layers deep into the organization, such that we no longer know everyone in our area and still must find ways to stay connected and visible. Being a voice of connection can come in many forms. Some of the ways I've seen others do this effectively:

- **Increase your skill as a storyteller.** Stories make our points more memorable and salient. They can enliven a keynote address or an all-hands meeting, drive home a point we're making in a presentation, or help to close a large deal or transaction.

- **Thank and acknowledge.** Our teams and colleagues often go to great lengths to ensure that deliverables are met, revenues are strong, and customers are satisfied. When we use our voice of connection, we remember to express gratitude to a team that worked through the holidays to close on the financials at the end of the quarter, or we remember to loop back with a colleague who made a valuable introduction or referral for us.

- **Make time for a few minutes of ice-breaking or rapport-building at the start of a conversation or meeting.** So often, we want to get right down to business, so we skip the niceties or pleasantries that help to build relationships with others. Where possible, and especially with colleagues who value that kind of connection, spend a couple of minutes to connect before diving into the work. On days where you're pressed for time, state that up front and transparently, so as not to create any misunderstandings. You can say something like: "I'm a little crunched for time today, so it would be great if we could dive right in."

Discovering and developing your voice as a leader is the work of a lifetime. The key is to stay open to an increasingly wide array of new situations and people. Use each situation as an opportunity to access more parts of your voice, rather than having a one-size-fits-all approach. Bring your voices of character, context, clarity, curiosity, and connection as the moment or situation warrants. Through this kind of learning and growth, not only will you increase your inner confidence and resilience, but you will also inspire the confidence of others around you in a more authentic and impactful way.

Adapted from content posted on hbr.org, January 10, 2018 (product #H043HT).

SECTION TWO

Speak Out on Sexual Harassment

4

Why Things Aren't Better Yet

A conversation with Marianne Cooper

Since #MeToo became a household term, a lot of people have been trying to make work a safer place for everyone. But organizational change is slow, and it's not always easy for individual employees to respond to and prevent sexual harassment.

Here are a few telling figures about the state of sexual harassment in corporate America. Thirty-five percent of women report having experienced it. Thirty-eight percent say their company has updated or clarified its policies and procedures in the past year. Only 52% of women think reporting harassment would lead to a fair and effective investigation. This is all from "Women in the Workplace 2018," published annually by LeanIn.org and McKinsey & Company, after surveying tens of thousands of employees in the United States and Canada.

Amy Gallo spoke with Marianne Cooper, a senior research scholar at the VMware Women's Leadership Innovation Lab at Stanford University. Cooper, one of the authors of LeanIn.org and McKinsey & Company's "Women in the Workplace 2018" report, shared some findings with us.

AMY GALLO: How did you react to the finding that harassment is still quite prevalent?

MARIANNE COOPER: It's certainly depressing, but it's not surprising. We've known for some time that the prevalence of sexual harassment is quite high, higher than most people would probably expect. In the "Women in the Workplace" report, 35% of women report experiencing it. But the numbers can get much higher, depending on the jobs that you're looking at. Women working in the restaurant industry or in low-paid service jobs tend to experience it at a much higher rate.

AMY: I was somewhat hopeful that there would be some change based on #MeToo. Did you expect to see a difference?

MARIANNE: Well, it depends on which issue we're talking about. With the prevalence of sexual harassment, it takes a while for companies to put the right policies in place, to get the right practices, to enforce the policies that they do have, to really look into the belly of the beast and decide whether or not they're going to address it, and then address it. When looking at this from the perspective of social change, we've had a huge revolutionary watershed moment in which women and others are rising up and saying, "We're just not going to take it anymore." The powers that be need to start to change things, but there's a lag between people speaking up and acting out and then companies adopting different ways of organizing things at work.

AMY: Are you hopeful that in three, five, 10 years, we will see change based on what's happened with #MeToo?

MARIANNE: What I've seen is an interesting phenomenon in and of itself: You can give people data about a social problem, and they will see the data, but they will not change the way that they're behaving. The lack of women at the top of companies is a socially produced phenomenon. Sociologists, social psychologists, and other scholars have documented many different explanations for why we see the patterns that we see. You can just look at companies' budgets and tell where their priorities are. You're not going to fix systemic sexism when you barely have a diversity and inclusion team and you're not really providing support for that team. You're not going to fix this problem if you're not even tracking things like how many women and people of color are at different levels. How many women and people of color are getting promoted? What are your numbers on pay equity? Just like any other business objective, you should have a plan, a strategy, key milestones, and key indicators of success. That's the way to approach this. I don't see that happening.

AMY: Can you explain how women in leadership roles in organizations and the issue of sexual harassment are connected and why we're talking about them together?

MARIANNE: Sexual harassment is much more likely in environments dominated by men. It's also more likely to occur when you have few women in leadership. So, if you have more women in leadership, the data tends to find lower rates of sexual harassment. And there are probably a few different reasons why that happens, but often it can be that women in organizations have more power. If you think about really hypermasculine environments in which you have hypercompetitive team members undermining each other, you get problems like sexual harassment. There's a lot of these dynamics—*co-occur* is the technical term. When you have more women at the top, it tends to create a whole different environment.

AMY: Since #MeToo, the number of organizations that have talked about and revisited their policies has increased, right?

MARIANNE: If you'd ask, have they clarified their policy, only 60% of employees are saying that a company has done that. You would think in the wake of #MeToo, that would be 99% of employees. This again shows the real disconnect between our culture and our society and what's happening inside organizations. This disconnect is interesting and hard to explain. Companies usually have a sexual harassment policy, but there's a gap between what the policy states and what's happening on the ground. Putting it into practice is apparently difficult.

AMY: How do you explain the difference between what's happening outside organizations and society and what's happening inside corporations in particular?

MARIANNE: Employees do the work they're expected to do, the work that they get rewarded for. What this shows is that, for managers in particular, it is not a part of their performance objectives to ensure safe cultures, to make sure their teams are diverse, and to foster a diverse and inclusive climate inside a company. If that is not on your list of performance objectives, you're going to focus on whatever *is* part of your objectives. So, there's misalignment.

AMY: One of the interesting findings was that there was a discrepancy between how men and women perceive what their organizations are doing, how they are putting policies in place. How do you make sense of that disparity?

MARIANNE: We've seen it in many different ways in many different questions in the report. There's a his-and-her story of what's happening inside companies. For example, we asked, "If you reported sexual harassment, it would be . . . ." We gave people a variety of options to choose from. Fifty percent of women thought it would be effective, but 70% of men thought it would be effective. There's another question about whether disrespectful behavior toward women is quickly addressed. Only 30% of women said that's true versus about 50% of men. So, there are these really large gender gaps, which point to different experiences and perhaps a lack of understanding about all the different things that can create microaggressions or disrespectful behavior. Certain kinds of behavior are just not seen in the same way by some men and by some women.

AMY: Based on these findings, what would you like readers—especially those who are leaders—to take away?

MARIANNE: Well, I think they need to approach this problem like every other business objective. It matters from a bottom-line perspective, when you have a diverse team or a diverse organization, if you leverage that diversity; those teams and those organizations tend to perform better. It's also fundamentally a matter of fairness and equity. Women have been outpacing men in higher education since the early 1980s. They're now earning 57% of bachelor's degrees. This is not a supply problem. The problem is not just going to take care of itself. It requires active intervention.

The biggest gender gap in promotion is at that first step up from entry level to manager. Often we try to solve the problem, not its origin. So, while we do need to focus on women in leadership and high-potential women, we really need to focus on that first step up and making sure that we don't have large disparities throughout the pipeline and the organization. Keep track of that data. Monitor it. Try to figure out what's happening so that you can solve the problem and create change that's going to last long term in your organization.

AMY: You mentioned that only 50% of women think reporting would be effective. Based on what you're seeing in this study, what advice would you give women who are thinking about reporting sexual harassment?

MARIANNE: When you look at the arc of history on this issue, this is a much better time than we've ever had. More women are speaking up and are being believed. More organizations are realizing that they have a serious problem and need to address it. So, all those elements are very important and favorable to speaking up.

The sad truth, though, is that women who report are often subjected to retaliation. So, the best thing to do if you're experiencing sexual harassment is to get as much information as possible so that you can make the most informed decision that you can. That means talking to a lawyer, figuring out what your company's policy is and how to report. Usually a company has outlined a procedure somewhere or somebody knows the steps involved in reporting. Document everything so that you have a record of what happened. Who was there? Did someone else observe it? Make sure you keep that documentation of dates, not at work, but at home. If you're suddenly retaliated against, you will still have access to your record. Keep a copy of your personnel file to avoid being discredited. Have your ducks in a row. Legal advice is always important.

But if no one speaks up, we can't move forward. So when someone speaks up, support them, and create a fair process for a thorough investigation. If a woman speaks up and her company shuts her down, or her company makes her sign a nondisclosure agreement, it's going to silence other women. What women and other people are saying right now is we're going to keep speaking up, but we have to be in solidarity with one another. My biggest worry is that this huge watershed moment won't get us as far as it could unless we stick together. Because really the only counterweight to this is women and other allies sticking together.

AMY: Can you help me make sense of why things aren't different? It's a frustrating feeling. How do you deal with that frustration yourself, as someone who's steeped in this?

MARIANNE: Sexism, misogyny, and racism are deeply embedded in our culture. They're baked into processes. People speaking up doesn't automatically undo that. There are systems of cultural beliefs about women making these things up. If we're just talking about sexual assault, for example, there have been studies about false accusations. There's just as many false accusations of sexual assault as other kinds of things. But there are larger beliefs that somehow people are not telling the truth, that they're out for their own social gain. It's really hard to dispel that and come to terms with this devalued view of women. A lot of people don't think that some of these things are that big a deal, when really they are. So, we're in a cultural moment of change in which new norms have to be established and enforced. Whose voices are believed? Who gets to speak their truth? All of those things are deeply tied to sexism, racism, and classism.

At the core, this is a fundamental, revolutionary moment about who gets to speak and who gets to be heard. And that doesn't get resolved in a short time. We're asking a lot of people in power to share, and historically that doesn't happen easily. Asking nicely doesn't usually lead to change. It's women and other people holding the powers that be accountable, putting their feet to the fire and saying, "It's great that you've signed whatever pledge or whatever else you're doing. Let's see what's happening on the ground." Almost every organization and institution would have to change for us to see real reductions in prevalence. But we're in a better place than we've ever been. Once they really believe that it's happening and understand the size of it, people act. So, hopefully we're at a tipping point. I don't think it's going to be significantly better in 18 months, but maybe in my children's lifetime.

Adapted from "Why Things Aren't Better, Yet," Women at Work *podcast, season 3, episode 9, June 10, 2019.*

5

Has Sexual Harassment at Work Decreased Since #MeToo?

by Stefanie K. Johnson, Ksenia Keplinger, Jessica F. Kirk, and Liza Barnes

Before #MeToo went viral, we surveyed 250 working women in the United States about the pervasiveness of sexual harassment in their workplaces and how it impacts them at work; we also interviewed 31 women in the U.S. about their individual experiences. We conducted a second survey after #MeToo, of 263 women, and we reconnected with some of the women we previously interviewed to see whether they've seen changes or have changed their views. The survey was meant to gather quantitative evidence about changes since #MeToo, and the interviews were meant to provide insight into why and how the changes occurred.

We measured sexual harassment along three dimensions: gender harassment, unwanted sexual attention, and sexual coercion. Gender harassment involves negative treatment of women that is not necessarily sexual but may include things like a supervisor or coworker making sexist remarks, telling inappropriate stories, or displaying sexist material. Unwanted sexual attention includes coworker or supervisor behaviors such as staring, leering, ogling, or unwanted touching. Sexual coercion includes bribing or pressuring women to engage in sexual behavior. We also measured participants' self-esteem and self-doubt, to see how these correlated with their experiences.

What Has Changed

What did we find?[1] In terms of what has changed, we saw that fewer women in our sample reported sexual coercion and unwanted sexual attention following the #MeToo movement. In 2016, 25% of women reported being sexually coerced, and in 2018, that number had declined to 16%. Unwanted sexual attention declined from 66% of women to 25%.

In contrast, we noticed an increase in reports of gender harassment, from 76% of women in 2016 to 92% in 2018. This data suggests that while blatant sexual harassment—experiences that drive many women out of their careers—might be declining, workplaces may be seeing a "backlash effect," or an increase in hostility toward women.

When we examined women's feelings of self-esteem and self-doubt, we found an increase in self-esteem and a decrease in self-doubt since 2016. More important, the relationship between unwanted sexual attention and both of these outcomes (lower self-esteem, higher self-doubt) was weaker in 2018. Likewise, the relationship between gender harassment and the outcomes decreased. We believe that the knowledge that so many women experience sexual harassment has tempered its deleterious effects on self-doubt and self-esteem.

Social psychological theories suggest that stigmatizing experiences, like sexual harassment, can be damaging to self-esteem, especially because the stigmatized individuals fear that they are alone and share in the blame for their mistreatment. Knowing how pervasive sexual harassment is, and hearing other women's experiences, can help buffer one's self-esteem from the stigma of harassment.

The women we interviewed told us that the #MeToo movement helped them realize that they were not alone in their experiences. A marketing executive in her late thirties explained, "I started seeing [#MeToo posts] coming in, and I was just like, 'Oh my gosh, they're being so brave. Telling very personal stories that I never knew about' . . . It isn't like I'm vindicated; it is more, I'm validated."

What Companies and Managers Can Do

What should companies and managers be doing? On the most basic level, we need to continue to highlight the importance of preventing sexual harassment. Within organizations, human resource departments need to maintain this as a priority by offering bystander intervention training, having clear zero-tolerance policies on sexual harassment, and responding dutifully to complaints.

Several women told us that it is imperative that human resource departments remain vigilant in responding to concerns around harassment. One woman said, "I think that it's more and more common for people to say something when they see something, or feel uncomfortable . . . The bigger issue isn't somebody saying something in the first place; it's the response from an employer when they learn that one of their employees is sexually harassing another." Managers can also ensure that women and men feel safe to speak up about harassment.

Organizations should also pay attention to gender harassment, including bullying and sexist comments about women. One woman told us she believes that women who have been empowered by #MeToo to call out inappropriate behavior have faced more hostility among coworkers. It is important that organizations are aware of this, as constant exposure to gender harassment can be just as damaging to women as the most egregious forms of sexual harassment.[2]

Offering training that is focused on this issue, as well as on microaggressions and unconscious bias, could be useful not only for encouraging civil behavior but also for empowering peers and leaders to step in when they see bullying or harassing behavior in the workplace. It can be stressful for a woman to stand up to sexist comments when they are directed at her, but it can be a lot easier for a bystander to step in and defuse the situation.

These efforts will be the most successful if organizations are able to enlist male allies in the gender equity conversation (see section 4). Men need to hear the message that taking these issues seriously is not an accusation against them, but rather is a mutual effort to create an environment of respect in the workplace. I like the Twitter campaign #yesallwomen, which is intended to remind men (and women) that no one believes all men are sexual harassers, but that all women do experience harassment in their careers. As one woman told us, "[#MeToo] is bringing out a community of men who are supportive of women and supporting them in whatever challenging situations, whether it's to the extreme of the #MeToo movement or just down to, 'How do I get equal representation and equal voice in a meeting?' It's developing a network of men who are comfortable saying, 'Yeah, I'll be your supporter, and I can speak out on your behalf.'"

And we cannot forget the most vulnerable workers. Most efforts around gender equity and reducing sexual harassment in the workplace focus on full-time, salaried potential leaders. However, there is evidence that the people at greatest risk for harassment are gig workers, those making minimum wage (or server wages), and part-time or temp employees.[3] People in these roles are often the most powerless because they are not protected by EEOC laws. Creating a safer workplace means keeping everyone in mind. Greater legislation to protect nonemployees would be an obvious first step, but until that happens, gig workers and organizations can be proactive in putting antiharassment clauses in their contracts to increase worker protection. Gig workers can also use online platforms to crowdsource information about which organizations are safe.

While our results point to the benefits of #MeToo in reducing sexual harassment, we need to ensure that we maintain these changes, that women *and men* provide support for those who are harassed, and that vulnerable workers are not ignored. The goal of these efforts is continued progress on workplace equity, and this goal benefits all employees.

Adapted from content posted on hbr.org, July 18, 2019 (product #H0522T).

6

A Tool to Navigate the Gray Areas of Sexual Harassment

by Kathleen Kelley Reardon

The Time's Up movement was founded shortly after #MeToo gained momentum to foster fairness, safety, and equity for women in the workplace. Part of its purpose is to alter the power system that favors men and thereby provides a foundation for discrimination and hostility toward women.

The passion was palpable. A cultural shift had taken place, and not just for women. Men began to consider their roles; some engaged in soul searching, wondering if they'd done enough as bystanders to stop sexual misconduct directed at women. Others, however, felt threatened. They worried that the accusations against high-profile men leading to resignations and firings might happen to them. Some adopted the "Pence Rule" at work, refusing to meet with women alone.

In my experience working with leaders in organizations, much of this negative reaction to women's voices being raised stems from a lack of understanding about what exactly constitutes harassment. Because there is a lot of gray area when it comes to delineating mild to serious forms of gender-based offenses, confusion naturally clouds efforts to eradicate them—and questions abound. Where are the lines over which men should not step? How should men and women be handling comments and behaviors that are mildly—or deeply—offensive? When are resignation and firing appropriate?

In response to questions like these, I developed the spectrum of sexual misconduct at work (SSMW) to help people define and differentiate among types of gender-based offense.

A Spectrum to Define and Differentiate Gender-Based Offenses

The SSMW was derived from my interviews and interactions with hundreds of women in a wide variety of fields. It is intended as a blueprint for men, women, and organizations to use in becoming familiar with levels of offense that can harm work relationships and create or perpetuate hostile work environments.

Most important, the SSMW provides a means of talking about sexual misconduct—a way to halt backlash against women by formulating solutions. It also helps women decide when and how to respond to behaviors they see as offensive, whether minor or extreme. Organizations can use it as a framework to provide training that improves work culture and lowers the risk of conflict and legal action.

As you can see from figure 6-1, I used the term "sexual misconduct" to include mild and moderate forms of

FIGURE 6-1

The spectrum of sexual misconduct at work

Knowing where a behavior falls depends on the situation, history of the relationship, tone of delivery, and nonverbal actions.

1. **Generally not offensive**
   Common remarks on things such as hairstyle and dress
2. **Awkward/mildly offensive**
   Comments involving or implying gender distinctions unfavorable to women
3. **Offensive**
   Gender-insensitive or superior manner
4. **Highly offensive**
   Intentionally denigrating comments or behaviors
5. **Evident sexual misconduct**
   Behaviors that are crude or physically intrusive
6. **Egregious sexual misconduct**
   Behaviors involving coercion, sexual abuse, or assault

Source: Kathleen Kelley Reardon, professor emerita, University of Southern California Marshall School of Business.

offense, sexual harassment, and abuse. The lowest level on the spectrum ("Generally not offensive" behavior) is included because women repeatedly told me that some seemingly innocuous behaviors, such as commenting on a woman's looks or manner of dress, if accompanied by sexually toned glances or gestures, can be experienced as misconduct. Additionally, women I've interviewed believe such comments and behaviors, if repeated often enough, become offensive.

Decisions about which category a behavior falls into depend on the situation, history of the relationship, tone of delivery, and nonverbal behaviors. I can, however, provide some general examples to facilitate discussion. Comments like "You look nice today" or "I like your haircut" would most likely fall into the first category of "Generally not offensive." Whereas a comment such as "We can't speak frankly around you women anymore" is more likely to be interpreted as at least "Awkward/mildly offensive." Behaviors such as uninvited hugs or implying or stating that women are distracted by family likely move along the spectrum to "Offensive."

Jokes or implications about a woman's intellect or skills being limited due to her gender or comments on physical attributes made with the intention of embarrassing, insulting, or demeaning the target are examples of the "Highly offensive" category. Behaviors further along the spectrum toward "Evident sexual misconduct" include such behaviors as looking a woman up and down in a sexually suggestive manner or grabbing, touching, kissing, or otherwise ignoring a woman's expressed disinterest in an intimate relationship. At the far end of the spectrum, "Egregious sexual misconduct" includes behaviors such as pressing against a woman suggestively and threatening or implying career damage to a woman who refuses to engage in sex or sexual behavior. The placement of these examples may vary somewhat across teams adapting the spectrum for their own use, and teams may develop additional examples relevant to the culture in which they work.

Note that while the SSMW focuses on offensive behavior directed at women by men, sexual misconduct can take many forms. Certainly, a woman can be the offending party. An additional benefit of using the SSMW as a blueprint for discussions is that those other forms can be identified along with ways of effectively dealing with them.

How Companies Are Using the Spectrum

My goal in developing the SSMW was not to create a cut-and-dried, one-size-fits-all, static set of categories. I wanted to provide a working taxonomy that organizational teams and groups can adapt and make their own. Persuasion research shows that if people are involved in discussing different ways of looking at situations and developing rules for responses consistent with their views, they are more likely to be receptive to change.[1] Ideally, people at organizations will work together to provide additional examples of behaviors at each level of the spectrum as well as ways to effectively respond.

Organizations from law firms to tech companies to nonprofits have been using the spectrum. My advice to them—and to anyone who wants to implement it—is to treat the spectrum as a living document. Talk about what behaviors and examples should go where and why (see the sidebar "Using the Spectrum in Your Organization").

The experiences of companies using the spectrum have been encouraging. Katherin Nukk-Freeman, an attorney and partner at Nukk-Freeman & Cerra P.C., has used the spectrum in training employees and found that it can encourage an "upstander culture." By this she means a willingness on the part of women and men to address sexual misconduct and deal with it openly and constructively. Instead of ignoring incidents, Nukk-Freeman says, people are more willing to speak up.

David Lawrence, the chief collaborative risk officer at the Risk Assistance Network and Exchange, sees the SSMW as an essential tool for organizations to "understand the various and often nuanced ranges of sexual misconduct that can occur—as well as to find the necessary solutions from a risk management perspective that can protect an organization's reputation." He believes

Using the Spectrum in Your Organization

Here are a few scenarios to start the conversation using the spectrum in your team, division, or company. Bring people together with a proven facilitator who can keep the discussion away from naming particular people and placing blame. Discuss where on the spectrum each scenario belongs. Determine if the situation can be resolved on the spot. If so, what could be said to ensure it won't happen again? Which ones present teachable moments, and which are too far along the spectrum and so require interventions by senior management and/or HR?

- After inviting you to a meeting, a colleague notes that you'll be a great addition because you'll bring a "woman's gentle perspective."
- Your boss gives you an enthusiastic, tight hug after you tell him that you landed a client deal. He has never done this before.
- Several times, you've made clear to your manager that you don't want to go out with him. He tells you that's a bad career decision.
- A more senior person in your organization tells you that he's "taken an interest in you" and regularly insists you sit next to him at meetings,

(continued)

pulling your chair close. You overhear him tell your boss, with a smile that makes you uncomfortable, that he plans to mentor you.

- A coworker tells you that he had a dream about you last night. When you ask what it was about, he says, “You don’t want to know” and winks at you.
- Your boss tends to use his hands when he speaks. One time in an animated discussion, he throws his arms out wide—and accidentally touches your breast.
- A colleague requests a meeting with you but in a private place so “no one will get the wrong idea.”
- You come to work wearing a new dress. Your boss comments in passing that it looks nice on you.
- A colleague corners you at an off-site meeting. Others are watching. You try to edge away. He pulls you close and kisses you hard.
- You stand up at your desk. A male coworker looks you up and down and says to the amusement of others, “Nine point five.”
- You wear a slightly snug sweater to work and a coworker says, “You’ve been hiding your light under a bushel.” He appears to mean it as a compliment.

that too many organizations are underresponding. Some leaders think that certain conduct could never exist in their organizations. Others lay low or believe they've done enough about sexual misconduct. But, Lawrence says, "Organizations that don't provide employees with a way to talk about it, raise the issues early and share their experiences and perspectives, will remain on a slippery slope." He adds, "While they wring their hands, the problem can quickly metastasize."

Sandra Corelli, vice president at the training company Corporate Class Inc., based in Toronto, has worked in HR for over 18 years and has started using the spectrum in her trainings on gender differences. For her, the spectrum is useful in ensuring that the person who comes forward about sexual misconduct "feels heard and seen," since it captures the nuance found in so many of these situations. "A single comment or gesture may mean little, but a string of them can turn into a sentence"—perhaps with unintended offensive meaning, she says. Corelli advises that no senior manager take for granted that offenses on the spectrum aren't happening where they work.

Challenges to Using the Spectrum

Of course, using the SSMW presents challenges for some organizations. Speaking with U.S. congressional and senatorial staff members, for example, I found concern about being too visible on this issue, in part because they were afraid of creating a backlash. Another concern is that some colleagues have been asked to resign before their alleged misconduct could be assessed using a spectrum approach. If, after using the SSMW, they realized that they might have overreacted or, in other cases, underreacted, there would be many challenging questions to answer.

The SSMW might also be difficult to use in an organization where open conversations about challenging issues aren't the norm. Nukk-Freeman says that the spectrum would likely be more welcome in an "evolved organization" characterized by openness and flexibility.

The #MeToo movement escalated due to sexual misconduct in an industry known for a lack of such openness. I recently spoke with David Puttnam and Sandy Lieberson, award-winning producers and educators who described the film industry as especially challenging for women. Puttnam explained that even women who seemed secure at the top in the past have "always felt like they were looking over their shoulders," and Lieberson emphasized the "culture of fear" and lack of mentoring that hurt women's chances of long-term success. Such corporate cultures tend to go into lockdown when issues of sexual misconduct arise.

Talking about sexual misconduct may indeed bring up feelings that many individuals and organizations would just as soon avoid. But conflict is a part of change. The spectrum should be employed with facilitators—internal or external—who can manage discussions to avoid anger and help people focus on the future rather than the past.

What to Say to Stop Gender-Based Offenses in the Moment

In addition to helping organizations have more open conversations about what is and isn't inappropriate, I also wanted to help people develop a repertoire of responses they can employ on the spot when an offense occurs.

By empowering people to respond on their own, issues that could become legal problems can be dealt with between or among the parties involved. The following comments are samples that can be used to halt gender-based offenses; some are suited to lesser offenses and to people with styles that are not direct. Others get right to the point. Which you choose to use will depend on the situation and what feels right to you.

> "I'm taking a moment to be sure I heard you right."

> "This seems like a good time to take a break—to reflect on what was just said."

> "If I look perplexed, it's because I'm thinking about how to give you the benefit of the doubt."

"I suggest we step back for a moment, as something just went awry."

"Of all the things I thought you might say, that certainly wasn't one of them."

"If I said what I'm thinking, we'd both be out of line."

"For two people who respect each other, we're certainly off course today."

"Do you want to run that by me again in a less personal way?"

"Did you really say that?"

"I usually respond defensively to comments like that, so give me a moment."

"If I didn't know you, I'd think you were insulting me."

"I have a rule about comments like that one—I don't respond."

"Were you making a point or simply trying to amuse yourself at my expense?"

"You're funny sometimes, but not today."

The #MeToo movement highlighted the considerable risk to careers and organizations, and potential backlash against women as well as the need to make every effort to talk openly about sexual misconduct. The better our ability to articulate how and to what extent particular behaviors offend, the better the chances of women and men working effectively and equitably together. While these conversations are no doubt challenging, they are far superior to a black hole of silence. No good can come from that.

Adapted from "It's Not Always Clear What Constitutes Sexual Harassment. Use This Tool to Navigate the Gray Areas," on hbr.org, June 19, 2018 (product #H04EAD).

7

Why Sexual Harassment Programs Backfire

by Frank Dobbin and Alexandra Kalev

The term *sexual harassment* spread through academic circles in the 1970s and began to gain traction as a legal concept in 1977. That year the feminist legal scholar Catharine MacKinnon put forward the argument that workplace harassment constitutes sex discrimination, which is illegal under the Civil Rights Act of 1964. Federal judges had previously rebuffed this idea, but by 1978 three courts had agreed with MacKinnon, and in 1986 the Supreme Court concurred.

The watershed moment for the concept came in 1991, during the Supreme Court nomination hearings for Clarence Thomas, when Anita Hill accused Thomas of having sexually harassed her while she was his assistant at the Equal Employment Opportunity Commission. Hill's televised testimony rocketed sexual harassment into public awareness and prompted many women to come forward with their own stories. Recognizing the extent of the problem—and growing increasingly worried about their legal and public-relations exposure—many companies decided they had to address it. They moved fast. By 1997, 75% of American companies had developed mandatory training programs for all employees to explain what behaviors the law forbids and how to file a complaint, and 95% had put grievance procedures in place for reporting harassment and requesting hearings. Training and grievance procedures seemed like good news for employees and companies alike, and in 1998 the Supreme Court ruled in two separate cases that companies could protect themselves from hostile-environment harassment suits by instituting both.

For a couple of decades most organizations and executives felt good about this: They were dealing with the problem. But sexual harassment is still with us, as the #MeToo movement has made clear. Today some 40% of women (and 16% of men) say they've been sexually harassed at work—a number that, remarkably, has not changed since the 1980s.[1] In part that could be because women are now more likely to use the term "harasser" than "cad" for a problem boss. But given how widespread grievance procedures and forbidden-behavior training have become, why are the numbers still so high?

That's an important question, and we recently decided to try to answer it. We did so by taking a serious look at what happened at more than 800 U.S. companies, with more than 8 million employees, between the early 1970s and the early 2000s. Did the programs and procedures that these companies introduced make their work environments more hospitable to women? We focused in particular on how those initiatives affected the number of women in the managerial ranks. We tested two hypotheses: First, if the programs and procedures are working, they should reduce the number of current and aspiring female managers who leave their jobs because of sexual harassment—and thus we should find more women in management over time. Second, if the programs and procedures are backfiring, current and aspiring female managers should be leaving their jobs in even greater numbers, and the overall number of women in management should be declining.

Our study revealed some uncomfortable truths.[2] Neither the training programs that most companies put all workers through nor the grievance procedures that they have implemented are helping to solve the problem of sexual harassment in the workplace. In fact, both tend to increase worker disaffection and turnover. To us the takeaway seems clear: The programs and procedures that the Supreme Court favored in 1998 amount to little more than managerial snake oil. They are doing more harm than good.

We have to do better. The good news is that our study revealed ways in which we can.

The Trouble with Harassment Training

Does harassment training that focuses on forbidden behaviors reduce harassment? Apparently not. When companies institute this kind of training, our study revealed, women in management lose ground. To isolate the effects of these programs, we used advanced statistical techniques to account for other changes in a firm, its industry, and its state that might be affecting the numbers of women in management. We found that when companies create forbidden-behavior training programs, the representation of white women in management drops by more than 5% over the following few years. African American, Latina, and Asian American women don't tend to lose ground after such harassment training is instituted—but they don't gain it either. White women make up three-quarters of all women in management and half of all women in the workforce, so as a group they bear most of the training backlash.

Why would training designed to educate employees about harassment create a backlash? That seems counterintuitive. The problem is with how the training is presented. Typically it's mandatory, which sends the message that men have to be forced to pay attention to the issue. And it focuses on forbidden behaviors, the nitty-gritty, which signals that men don't know where the line is. The message is that men need fixing.

Start *any* training by telling a group of people that they're the problem, and they'll get defensive. Once that happens, they're much less likely to want to be a part of the solution; instead they'll resist. That's what happens with harassment training: Research shows that it actually makes men *more* likely to blame the victims and to think that women who report harassment are making it up or overreacting.[3] No surprise, then, that in a 2018 study carried out by the Pew Research Center, more than 30% of men said that false claims of sexual harassment are "a major problem." And no surprise that 58% of women who had been harassed said that not being believed is a major problem.

This dynamic plays out in predictable ways—one of which is that men, put on the defensive, make jokes about the training scenarios and about harassment itself. The phenomenon is so common that the writers of *The Office* devoted an entire episode to it. At one point Pam, the receptionist, wearily tells the camera, "Usually, the day we talk about sexual harassment is the day everyone harasses me as a joke."

What about men who are prone to harass? The reason we make training mandatory is to reach those men. Does training help them, at least? No. Research shows that men who are inclined to harass women before training actually become more accepting of such behavior after training.[4]

Even so, what do companies usually do when they find men culpable in a grievance process? Sentence them to more training. Six states, including California and New York, now require all employers to provide harassment training to all workers.

George Orwell, meet Franz Kafka.

Training Alternatives

If the typical harassment training leads to the loss of female managers and makes the bad guys a little worse, it's probably time to start thinking about more-effective types of training. We've identified two in our research.

Bystander-intervention training

This is the most promising alternative we've come across. Sharyn Potter and her team at the University of New Hampshire's Prevention Innovation Research Center have long conducted interesting experiments with it on college campuses and military bases, where harassment and assault are rampant. A dozen years ago they piloted a college bystander-intervention program that has since been used on more than 300 campuses. In 2011 it was adapted for the U.S. Army.

In their programs, Potter and her team start with the assumption that trainees are allies working to solve the problems of harassment and assault rather than potential perps. Everybody's job is to nip misbehavior in the bud. It's the "If you see something, say (or do) something" approach. Properly trained bystanders interrupt the sexual joke. They call out the catcallers. They distract the drunk pair who have just met but are set to leave the party together. The approach is surprisingly effective. Students and soldiers who have taken part in bystander training consistently report that it has helped them know what to do when they see signs of a problem. Most important, even months after the training, trainees are significantly more likely than others to report having intervened in real-life situations.

Word is getting out about the merits of bystander training. Potter now chairs a nonprofit that develops programs for organizations of all sorts. The U.S. Air Force has developed its own. When the city of New York mandated in 2018 that all employers provide harassment training, it also required them to cover bystander intervention and offered a model online program that is free to employers. Unfortunately, the whole program lasts only 45 minutes and covers five topics, including forbidden behaviors. That's a far cry from what studies have found to be effective for college students and military personnel: several hours of live training that focuses on bystander intervention.

Manager training

Training delivered exclusively to managers is also quite effective. In our study, companies that adopted distinct manager-training programs saw significant gains in the percentage of women in their managerial ranks, with white women rising by more than 6%, African American and Asian American women by 5%, and Latinas by 2%.

Manager training works because it presents harassment as a challenge that *all* managers must deal with. In that way it resembles bystander training. Participants, men and women alike, are encouraged to imagine what they might see *other* people doing wrong; the focus is deliberately not on what they themselves might do wrong. Trainers advise participants on how to recognize early signs of harassment and how to intervene swiftly and effectively to prevent escalation.

Our research shows that men pay attention during manager training. Why? In part because they feel they're being given new tools that will help them solve problems they haven't known how to handle in the past—and in part because they're assumed to be potential heroes rather than villains. Everybody's in it together, learning how to recognize and curb dubious behaviors in ways that will improve the overall work environment.

The Trouble with Grievance Procedures

The evidence on forbidden-behavior training is clear: It isn't helping us address the problem of workplace sexual harassment. But what about legalistic grievance procedures?

Every *Fortune* 500 company we've looked at has a grievance procedure. These procedures were first cooked up by lawyers to intercept victims who were planning to sue, and then were adapted to protect companies against suits by the accused. But they haven't improved the situation for women. After the companies in our study implemented them, in fact, the total number of women working in management declined.

The biggest declines occurred in companies with few female managers. That's because women are more likely than men to believe reports of harassment.[5] When there are few female managers to receive reports, victims who complain are sometimes given the third degree, which prompts them to quit. At companies with the fewest female managers to begin with (those in the lowest quartile), the introduction of harassment grievance procedures led to significant declines, over several years, of 14% among African American, 10% among Latina, and 10% among Asian American female managers. The negative effects were smaller at companies with more women in managerial roles, and they disappeared in organizations with the most. Numbers of white women in management weren't affected by grievance procedures.

Why did women of color suffer most? Studies show that they are significantly more likely than white women to be harassed at work. Because these women bear the brunt of harassment, as a group they file the most complaints—and, naturally, suffer the most when grievance procedures backfire.

But why do those procedures backfire? The answer, according to a variety of studies, is retaliation against victims who complain. One survey of federal workers found that two-thirds of women who had reported their harassers were subsequently assaulted, taunted, demoted, or fired by their harassers or friends of their harassers.

This kind of retaliation has long-term effects. Women who file harassment complaints end up, on average, in worse jobs and poorer physical and mental health than do women who keep quiet.[6] And retaliation may be the only thing many victims get after filing a grievance, because most procedures protect the accused better than they protect victims.

Part of the problem is that confidentiality rules are unenforceable and thus can't prevent retribution. Both the accused and their accusers are told that the complaint is confidential because the accused is innocent until proven guilty. Those accused often think they are free to tell their friends, and managers who hear complaints may also tell others, looking for either corroboration or support for the accused. No matter how word gets out, friends of the accused may retaliate. After an Ohio waitress complained of harassment, the female manager she told revealed her complaint to coworkers, who subjected the waitress to nonstop jokes.

Another part of the problem is evidentiary rules. Many companies use the "beyond a reasonable doubt" standard to determine guilt, not the lower "preponderance of evidence" standard that the courts use for harassment claims. That makes it nearly impossible to prove guilt without a confession or a witness. Even if the accused is found guilty, confidentiality generally applies to the ruling, and thus word doesn't get out that, say, women should steer clear of Jerry.

Yet another is a reluctance to punish perpetrators. Companies sometimes offer to transfer victims to other departments or locations, but they almost never actually transfer or fire the accused, because they worry that the accused will sue.[7] Instead they typically mandate more training. Many companies even keep verdicts secret from accusers, which can lead to a perverse outcome: A victim who has "won" her case sees her harasser roaming the halls, and believing that this means she has lost it, she becomes dispirited or frustrated or angry and decides to leave her job.

But victims who face retaliation often quit well before the process is complete. That's what happened in September 2019, after Broti Gupta, a writer for the CBS sitcom *Carol's Second Act*, complained of intimate touching by an executive producer with the network, which had just revised its complaint system to improve the treatment of accusers. HR went legalistic and approved new rules to keep producers and writers apart. Gupta quit, saying she'd been cut out of the creative process in retaliation. Margee Magee, a writer who took her side, told the *New York Times*, "All we wanted was for him to watch like a 45-minute harassment video. None of this had to happen."

The evidence is unambiguous: Our current grievance system puts victims at a distinct disadvantage, through unenforceable confidentiality rules, a high evidentiary bar, and punishments that leave harassers in place. Moreover, everybody knows that the system is rigged. That's why HR officers often counsel victims against filing grievances—and why studies show that only about one in 10 victims makes a formal complaint. The messages you can read in posts at #WhyIDidntReport say it all: *They won't believe me. They'll put me through a sham hearing. The guy will get off. He'll try to get back at me. His buddies will think I did something to deserve it.* Accusers have only two real options: report harassment and suffer the consequences, or don't report it.

It's a lose-lose situation.

Alternative Complaint Systems

If the current system isn't working, how can you and your organization do better? We've identified a few good options.

The ombuds office

This is an entity that sits outside the organizational chain of command and works independently to resolve sexual harassment complaints. An ombuds (formerly ombudsman) system is informal, neutral, and truly confidential—only the ombuds officer needs to know of the complaint. This approach has two advantages over the current system: It allows accusers to determine whether to make their complaints known to the accused, and it avoids legalistic hearings entirely.

Consider what happened at MIT, the first major employer in the United States to address the problem of sexual harassment directly. In 1973 the university created an ombuds office to handle harassment and related complaints, and by the early 1980s the office was receiving 500 complaints a year. In the 1980s, when the program was well established, more than 90% of those who took their claims to the office wanted an informal, confidential process; 75% worried that a formal complaint would bring reprisal, rejection, or the silent treatment from their bosses, coworkers, or even their own families, and said they didn't want their harassers punished—they just wanted the problem to stop.

MIT worked with complainants to give them what they wanted. As a result, the university today brings forward lots of complaints, many of which it resolves to the victims' satisfaction. According to Mary Rowe, a labor economist and adjunct professor of negotiation who served for 42 years as the head of MIT's ombuds office, employers who genuinely want to expose and address harassment in the workplace *must* offer this sort of alternative to formal grievance systems. Why? Because victims don't want to bring formal complaints, and only one in 100 complaints, Rowe says, can survive the rigors of a legalistic grievance process. If such a process is the only option, most victims simply won't come forward.

Ombuds offices have spread across academia, law firms, and major news organizations over the past few decades. To help resolve harassment problems, these offices should make explicit that employees can come to them confidentially with their claims and concerns. When the University of Pennsylvania announced that victims of harassment could use its existing ombuds office, complaints and resolutions jumped. These offices are becoming more popular in the rest of the corporate world: Thirteen percent of U.S. companies have them, to handle issues ranging from bullying to termination. Among these are American Express, The Cheesecake Factory, McKinsey, Nike, Chevron, Mars, and Uber. The Cheesecake Factory created its office in response to sexual harassment complaints in 2009. In 2017, after an Uber employee published a scathing blog about the company's culture of harassment, Uber hired the former U.S. attorney general Eric Holder to investigate. Holder recommended creating an ombuds office to encourage employees to bring problems forward, and Uber's board did just that. The rise of #MeToo has brought a sea change in the attitudes of executives: *See no evil* has been replaced by *Bring it on*, as they realize that it's better to know about problems than to pretend they don't exist.

What's most important about the ombuds system is that it puts victims in the driver's seat. If they don't want the accused to know they're talking, that's OK—the ombuds can hear them out confidentially and help them think through their options. Ombuds offices hold no formal hearings, are guided by no rules of evidence, and impose no restrictions on discussing the problem with others. Moreover, by tracking complaints by department and location, they can identify problem spots that need attention and alert leaders. They track complaints more effectively than grievance officers can, because people actually bring complaints to them.

Setting up an ombuds office isn't hard. You need ground rules for complaint handling, which a professional officer can help you design, working along International Ombudsman Association guidelines. (A tip: You should be explicit about the fact that the ombuds will help with harassment.) You can even turn to one of the Silicon Valley startups that now offer online complaint systems. One of them, tEQuitable, operates a virtual ombuds office. Employers can subscribe to the service, which is confidential and gives their employees access to written advice online. If they need more than that, the company makes trained experts available for phone conversations. It doesn't report individual harassment complaints to employers, but it sends aggregate stats to executives, allowing them to identify hot spots. Corporate ombuds offices do the same.

Voluntary dispute resolution

For an alternative that falls somewhere between a formal grievance procedure and an ombuds office, consider a dispute-resolution system that relies on mediation. In this model, mediators hear claims, notify the accused, and try to find solutions that satisfy both sides. Some employers use professional mediators; others train their own workers to do the job. The system is less adversarial than a legalistic grievance procedure. This often suits victims, many of whom simply want their harassers to cut it out. But the victim must feel comfortable being identified to the accused, and both parties must be committed to finding a solution. Obviously, this approach doesn't work for the most egregious cases of harassment, for which the only sensible solution is to fire the perpetrator.

The U.S. Postal Service has long done interesting work with dispute resolution for discrimination and harassment complaints. For a while it experimented with outside professional mediators, and later it trained employees to do the job. Both options have worked well.

Here's how the USPS system works: After an accuser has filed her (or his) complaint and submitted a request for mediation, the accused is required to come to an initial meeting with the mediator, who in some cases is joined by a union rep as co-mediator. Participation is entirely voluntary for the accuser, and the accused may opt out of mediation after that first meeting. Mediation sessions are scheduled within two to three weeks and typically last three or four hours. Most participants feel good about how these sessions are conducted. The USPS has done exit surveys of all participants without breaking out accused and accusers, on the dispute-resolution principle that no party is on trial. They show that more than 90% of respondents are satisfied with their mediator's impartiality and with how they were treated during the process, and at least 60% are satisfied with the outcome. This alternative system led to a four-year decline of more than 30% in *formal* discrimination and harassment filings.

The advantage of voluntary dispute resolution is that accusers can decide at key points in the process whether to proceed. Once the process is initiated, if they feel the accused isn't engaging in good faith, or that the complaint needs to be handled in a more legalistic way, they can bow out and file a formal grievance.

An option to avoid

Mandatory arbitration is all the rage today in Silicon Valley and on Wall Street. When an employer adopts mandatory arbitration, all current employees and new hires are required to sign away the right to sue for any employment-related dispute, including claims of harassment. In exchange they are promised that any claim they file will be turned over for independent review to an external arbitrator who will hear both sides of the dispute and render a binding decision.

That may sound like dispute resolution, but it's far from it. Signing the arbitration contract means agreeing to keep any dispute confidential, to abide by arbitrators' decisions, and to refrain from taking employment disputes to court. If victims feel that arbitration isn't working, they have no recourse to a formal grievance system. And they don't choose the arbitrator, which may put them at a disadvantage: Because arbitrators hope to be hired again by the company, they may be reluctant to find it seriously at fault. If an arbitrator had ordered a California hospital chain to pay a harassment victim $168 million, as a federal court did in 2012, would the chain still be using that arbitrator?

In 2018 the New York State Legislature decided that employers shouldn't be able to require employees to sign away their right to sue under the Civil Rights Act, and it outlawed mandatory arbitration. But in 2019 a federal judge overrode that decision. So mandatory arbitration remains legal, and the number of companies requiring it is on the rise. By a recent estimate, more than a fifth of private-sector workers are now subject to mandatory arbitration.

Employees are pushing back, however. In late 2018, 20,000 Google employees walked out in protest, and in response Google agreed to end mandatory arbitration for sexual harassment cases. Then, in early 2019, the company ended *all* mandatory arbitration. Perhaps that will spur other companies to follow suit. But to date mandatory arbitration is the only option of the three listed above that has really caught on. That's not because it serves victims well but because it does the best job of protecting companies from litigation.

Will either of the more promising alternatives catch on? As long as the courts require grievance procedures, companies won't scrap them in favor of those alternatives. That's fine, because victims should always have a formal grievance system available as a last resort. But everybody would surely be better off if most harassment claims were addressed through a live or virtual ombuds office or a dispute-resolution system.

Changing the Culture

The changes we propose address shortcomings of the programs that the Supreme Court backed in 1998. But reducing harassment will require more than that. It will require changing the culture of your organization so that fighting harassment becomes part of your mission. You'll need to engage as many people as possible in the effort and create systems of accountability that get everyone involved in oversight.

Three tools offer promising ways to do that: train-the-trainer programs that turn employees into harassment experts; harassment task forces that put employees in charge of diagnosing problems and designing solutions; and openly published numbers so that everyone can track progress.

Train-the-trainer programs

Employees who volunteer to be trained as harassment trainers tend to become leaders committed to changing the culture. This approach is less expensive than using outside trainers, and it's much more effective than tick-the-box online courses.

Promisingly, it's getting some traction. Sharyn Potter's team at the University of New Hampshire uses a train-the-trainer model to address assault and harassment on college campuses. The University of Michigan has developed a fine-tuned model as part of its diversity-recruitment training. The U.S. Air Force has adopted a train-the-trainer model to deal with sexual assault, dating violence, and domestic violence throughout its ranks. Whether you train 10 trainers or 1,000, you've created a group of experts committed to change. If you hire a train-the-trainer organization, however, choose carefully: Some still spend most of their time on the failed forbidden-behavior curriculum.

Harassment task forces

When we conducted research on diversity programs, we discovered that establishing a task force is the single best way to improve diversity in the workplace. It also promises to help curb harassment by engaging more people. A CEO might commission a harassment task force and ask department chiefs to join it or send a lieutenant. The task force can look at HR data on harassment complaints, interview people across the company about their experiences, study company data on what kinds of workers are quitting, and more. Once the members have figured out what and where their company's specific problems are, they can brainstorm solutions and take them back to their own departments. Maybe they'll decide that work teams need to be mixed up so that women aren't so often outnumbered. Maybe they'll decide that the company needs to get more women involved in recruitment or more men involved in conducting harassment training.[8]

The beauty of this approach is that it allows solutions to be tailored to the needs of a given company. Who better to dream up those solutions than people who know the workplace and the culture? And how better to align your managers and employees with the goal of stemming harassment than by putting them on the task force? That's a lesson straight out of Psych 101: The best way to convert people to your cause is to get them to help you with it.

Published numbers

There's something to the adage "You can't manage what you can't measure"—or in this case, "what you *don't* measure."

If you publish data that exposes a problem, managers will focus on it, and solving the problem will become part of the culture. Uber was acting on this principle when it published the number of sexual assaults that allegedly took place in its vehicles in 2018. Tech firms have acted on it by publishing data on diversity in their workforces, and Intel recently published pay data for men and women, whites, and people of color. Emilio Castilla, of MIT's Sloan School of Management, has conducted cutting-edge research demonstrating the efficacy of this approach when it comes to pay. Your ombuds office could post the number of complaints, broken down by department. An annual employee survey could surface problems by department and location. Most managers have no idea how their own departments are faring, because people rarely file formal complaints. Shining a light on where problems lie can change the culture.

Conclusion

Courts have been allowed to dictate how companies handle harassment for too long. Rates of harassment haven't budged for decades. The work that we and others have done suggests that we can't solve the problem by tagging all men as potential harassers in training sessions or by making victims navigate a complaint system designed to prevent the accused from suing. The research suggests that what's most helpful is to design training that treats all workers as victims' allies and gives them problem-solving tools, and to design complaint systems that provide the typical victim with a quick response that doesn't spark retaliation.

In the end, though, we need to change corporate cultures to get more people involved in solving the problem. Culture is ultimately created by leaders. They need to publicly take responsibility for the problem and try to solve it on their teams, setting an example for all managers. Increasing the numbers of female managers and executives may help as well, because women are less likely to react negatively to training and more likely to believe victims who come forward with complaints. That might encourage victims to come forward and make it more likely that they get satisfaction from the complaint process.

Reprinted from Harvard Business Review, *July–August 2020 (product #S20031).*

8

Why Open Secrets Exist in Organizations

by Insiya Hussain and Subra Tangirala

When the *New York Times* broke the scandal of media mogul Harvey Weinstein's apparent decades-long pattern of sexual abuse and harassment, the story came as a shock to the public. However, as details emerged, it became clear that Weinstein's transgressions were not unknown to Hollywood insiders. They were, in fact, an "open secret."

This raises the question: Why do issues remain open secrets in organizations where multiple employees know about a problem or a concern, but no one publicly brings it up? We explore this in a set of studies published in the *Academy of Management Journal*.[1]

We found that as issues become more common knowledge among frontline employees, the willingness of any individual employee to bring those issues to the attention of the top management *decreased.* Instead of speaking up, what we observed among our participants was something like the *bystander effect,* defined by *Psychology Today* as a psychological phenomenon describing how people stay on the sidelines as passive bystanders, waiting for others to act rather than do something themselves.

The bystander effect can be understood with an example: Imagine Jane, a member of an engineering team at a company. The top management of the company is eager to release a product to the market before competitors mimic it. However, a bug in the product has been uncovered, and someone needs to raise the issue. When Jane is the only member of the team who is aware of the issue, she would feel a personal responsibility to alert her managers of the problem. But, when her team members—John, Jack, and Julia—also know about the bug, Jane might feel that approaching leadership isn't solely her responsibility. She becomes less likely to speak up, and for the very same reason, John, Jack, and Julia are also less likely to do so.

Indeed, our research shows that when multiple individuals know about an issue, each of them experiences a *diffusion of responsibility* or the sense that they need not personally take on any costs or burden associated with speaking up. They feel that others are equally knowledgeable and, hence, capable of raising the issue with top management. They find it convenient to psychologically pass on the accountability of speaking up to others, and this makes them less likely to speak up themselves.

Considered from this perspective, it starts to make more sense why problems—such as harassment and abusive supervision—can remain unaddressed for so long without anyone taking action. Voicing such issues is, after all, risky, as individuals can often be punished or put down for speaking up.[2] Thus, when Jane, John, Jack, and Julia all know about the same concern, each tends to wait for one of the others to take on the risks of speaking up and feels less personally guilty or duty-bound to bring up the issue themselves. The bystander effect kicks in, and diffusion of responsibility prevents issues from percolating up to managers.

Our Research

We found these results consistently across three studies. Our first study was in the India branch of a *Fortune* 500 electronics company in which we surveyed 132 employees (from 25 teams) and their managers, about their work and how often they spoke up in the team. We carefully mapped out the workflow in each team. This allowed us to track the extent to which each employee in the sample had opportunities to observe the same work-related problems as their peers. We also asked the managers to report on the extent to which their employees raised ideas or concerns with them.

We found that the more employees observed problems that they thought were also observed by their peers, the less willing they were to speak up to their managers about those problems. When multiple employees knew about an issue, each one became less willing to speak up about it.

In the second study, we conducted a behavioral experiment with 163 undergraduate students at an eastern U.S. university. Students read about an issue concerning the lack of shuttle buses between distant campus buildings. Students then had the option to raise this issue to the university senate, which would involve writing to the senate and potentially meeting with a director at the senate to discuss the issue. We then randomly assigned students to either a condition in which they learned that their peers were aware of the issue or a condition in which they learned that they were the only one aware of the issue.

As we expected, students who believed their peers were also aware of the issue reported a greater sense of diffusion of responsibility to speak up relative to those who believed they were the only ones aware of the issue. In fact, those who believed they were the only ones aware of the issue were *2.5 times more likely to volunteer* to personally raise the issue with the senate.

In a third study, we conducted another behavioral experiment with 440 working adults, who read a realistic scenario about a problem with a product they were creating in their unit. We again found that participants were less likely to report being willing to speak up about the problem to company management when their peers also knew about the problem, because they felt psychologically less responsible for raising the concern.

In all three studies, our results held even when we statistically controlled for several other factors, such as whether participants felt it was safe to speak and whether they thought speaking up would make a difference. For instance, even when employees reported feeling confident about their ability to speak up, they did not raise issues when they knew that their peers were equally aware of them.

What Managers Should Take Away

Our research suggests that the bystander effect can be real and strong in organizations, especially when problems linger out in the open to everyone's knowledge. So if you're wondering why that particular boss seems to get away with bad behavior, or why no one has spoken up about an obvious glitch in a company product, consider whether everyone—including yourself—might be waiting for someone else to take action.

What can managers do to avoid the bystander effect so that problems don't go unresolved? A few key recommendations:

- Managers should tell employees that their voices are not redundant and that they need to share their opinions even if others have the same information. Managers might adjust the familiar injunction as follows: "If you see something, say something (*even if others see the same thing*)."
- The bystander effect occurs because the work culture of many organizations encourages passing the buck and blending into the crowd rather than individual responsibility. Employees are afraid of standing up and speaking truth to power. Managers who explicitly reward rather than punish acts of individual courage can get their employees off the sidelines to act as engaged citizens at the workplace.

Steps such as these can help organizations avoid the burgeoning of "open secrets" and of unresolved yet commonly known problems that no one seems to do anything about.

Adapted from content posted on hbr.org, January 14, 2019 (product #H04QN7).

9

How to Conduct Difficult Conversations About Sexual Harassment

A conversation with Sarah Pierson Beaulieu

Companies are still sorting out the right policies to put in place and how to enforce them effectively. But no matter what companies do, employees of all genders need the skills and confidence to respond to sexual harassment.

Amy Bernstein, Amy Gallo, and Nicole Torres spoke with Sarah Pierson Beaulieu, author of *Breaking the Silence Habit: A Practical Guide to Uncomfortable Conversations in the #MeToo Workplace*. She trains leaders and employees on how to respond to and prevent inappropriate behavior in their companies. Beaulieu talked us through what to say in various difficult situations at work.

AMY GALLO: What stood out to you about Marianne Cooper's findings (discussed in chapter 4)? Are you seeing the same thing in terms of not much progress being made since #MeToo?

SARAH PIERSON BEAULIEU: I am. One challenge is that these issues are slow moving. But culture is conversation. When you teach people how to talk about the culture that permits sexual harassment to occur, they are willing to learn how to do things differently.

Sometimes these conversations will focus on incidents of sexual harassment that already occurred. They'll center on rules about what happened, what could have happened, how it was handled. And those kinds of conversation are important for creating the changes that need to happen in our society. But the conversations that will really create a safer and more inclusive culture for everyone are those day-to-day conversations we have with each other as individuals.

NICOLE TORRES: What skills do we need to be better at identifying when something bad is happening?

SARAH: Empathy: seeing the world through somebody else's eyes. There are huge differences in the ways that people experience the same situation or conversation. So, somebody might feel like gosh, that's just a hug. Who cares? But for somebody else, it's the 17th unwanted hug that they've gotten that day.

There is also an expectation that you should speak up when you know exactly the right thing to say and that it will feel great when you do it. The truth is that it's going to feel horribly uncomfortable. Your heart is going to pound and you're going to question whether you're saying the right thing. It doesn't matter what gender you are. People need to get comfortable with that and have a chance to practice those conversations ahead of time. But a lot of the current compliance training is designed to show what harassment is or isn't.

We need to create an environment where people aren't getting shamed for asking questions like "Is it OK to give somebody a compliment?" If you've got a question, let's unpack it. Often there's a misunderstanding about intention versus impact or holding two things to be true at the same time. A lot of the questions I get are about reporting and understanding why it's so hard to report. But if you don't report, organizations can't take action against harassment. Those are the uncomfortable aspects.

AMY BERNSTEIN: When you find yourself dealing with clueless or possibly even criminal men, how do you get to the point where you can actually say something? How do you make that leap?

SARAH: It takes a lot of practice. An intervention conversation when you are the victim of harassment is an unrealistic expectation for people. We need to ask ourselves, does this person have any friends who could intervene on their behalf? Is the person the only one who's being impacted by this situation? Are there other people I can bring in off the sidelines?

AMY G: Tell us about a time when you've brought in other people.

SARAH: I was traveling for a speaking engagement, and I was very tired. I decided to have dinner and a drink in a bar. I just wanted to enjoy the view, but a man started speaking to me. At first, I said, "No, no thank you." "How's your dinner?" he said. I said, "It's great." I went back to my writing. He persisted. I turned to him and said, "Look, I'm just trying to enjoy my dinner alone." He said, "Oh, I'm not trying to bother you." Then he started commenting on my appearance. "You look like an actress. What do you do for work?" I told him I train workplaces on sexual harassment. It still did not deter him. At this point I noticed that there were two other gentlemen sitting to my right who were noticing the interaction, and at some point they smirked a little bit. So I knew I wasn't alone in that situation. Ultimately, I turned to these two men and I asked, "What keynote are you going to tomorrow at your conference?" I didn't know if they were going to a conference. I just made it up. And they started engaging in a conversation with me. That stopped the harassment from continuing. It allowed me to have a little bit of breathing room. It turned out the bartending staff had been trained, so when this guy tried to buy me a drink, the bartender refused. When I asked for my check, they just gave it to me. I paid and then I complained to the manager.

AMY B: After that whole scenario ended, did you talk to the other two guys you mentioned?

SARAH: I did. On my way out, I stopped and said, "Hey, thank you. What you did was perfect because you stopped him; I could tell you didn't want that to happen." I told them they got an A+ for bystander intervention. When I got back to my room, I was still very energized about the whole thing. The bystanders had been wearing polo shirts with logos on them. So, I looked up their company and emailed the CEO. I wrote, "I just want to thank you because you have two loving employees who were out representing your company well. Could you please also send along my thanks to their high-school teachers, their parents, anybody that they worked for, any company that they worked for before you, because they did a good job representing."

AMY G: One of the things you said strikes me: It's an unrealistic expectation for someone who is the subject of the harassment to intervene. In those moments when it's happened to me, I feel completely frozen and completely alone. So, your example is about making eye contact with other people, knowing you're going to need help and looking for the helpers in the room.

SARAH: Absolutely. You are not alone. I was debriefing the conversation with a male colleague the next day, who said he's seen that situation play out many times and often doesn't know what to say or how to say it and doesn't want to seem like he's trying to make a pass at somebody. There's just awkwardness. But if we had more proactive conversations ahead of time about how if you're at a bar and see somebody who's being harassed, you can buy the guy a drink and send it to the other end of the bar. You can make up a conversation. You can ask, "Are you OK? Do you need any help?" You can alert the bartender. People can do lots of things in a bar. But there are plenty of similar workplace examples.

NICOLE: How would that be different in a workplace? Isn't it harder when you know everyone involved?

SARAH: It absolutely makes it harder. That's why practice conversations help people understand and get on the same page about those dynamics. I hear a lot about younger sales representatives who are having dinner with an important client, and there's some kind of inappropriate interaction, like very close talking or putting a hand on somebody's back or shoulder. Sometimes people assume that this young woman has it under control, but there are six other colleagues there. Certainly a conversation can happen, and an intervention can take place at that dinner table. But most of the intervention happens in conversations that take place before you get there. If you're a salesperson, has your manager told you that you don't have to accept inappropriate behavior and that they always want to know about it? What do your sales incentives look like? Do you know if the CEO would make a call to the client's CEO and tell them that they've got a representative who has a problem? When you run through some of those scenarios ahead of time, people feel more empowered in that moment because they know that there are helpers . But you want to know if somebody is a helper before that incident takes place, not when an incident is happening.

AMY G: But, I've heard a lot of men say, "I just couldn't figure out what was going on. It wasn't clear if she wanted help, if she was receptive to the attention, and I wasn't sure that if I stepped in, I would be making her feel weak."

SARAH: The intervention is on the culture, not on the person. I don't want to be working in an environment where this kind of behavior goes unchecked. If I know ahead of time, for example, that you're a handshake person and somebody's going to hug you, then my responsibility is to say, "No. She doesn't want a hug. Don't hug her." I have called out men in a humorous way, like, oh, no hug for the guy? Just to make people aware of what they do.

AMY B: Do you report to HR? What should you expect?

SARAH: Let's say you walk by a manager's office late at night, and you see the manager leaning over, very close, in an awkward way, with a more junior employee. You decide you want to do the right thing but don't have the skill to intervene. In this case, you decide to go to HR and report it. Most often, HR will have a conversation with them. You do the right thing, from my perspective, by reporting the incident, but maybe the two people are engaged in a consensual affair. Maybe they told the same story about what happened and maybe they told different stories. Maybe the manager is a close toucher, but the junior person didn't want to report it or confirm that, in fact, that was what happened.

You may not see any outcome, and sometimes that's really frustrating, especially if you don't know how these kinds of reports typically go down. You're not always going to get a report back. Then you have to work with the two people involved. So, you may feel the manager is looking at you while you're getting coffee. You may wonder whether they know that you were the one who said something.

You have a number of choices. You could walk by, get in your car, go home, and hope that the junior employee in the office will have the power to report whatever was happening. Talking to the person is another choice, and perhaps a good first conversation to figure out what you saw. But the reporting is challenging.

AMY G: I heard about an organization where several people went to HR to complain about a particular man's behavior. Then, HR and management said they investigated and the investigation was over. The man was still there. What should those people have expected from HR?

SARAH: I'm very careful not to second-guess somebody else's decisions. However, I would be curious about what was reported and documented. Was there some accountability that was not visible? Termination is very visible, but a warning is not. This person may have been warned about future reports and potential termination. But nobody wants to report when there's this whole whisper network around this person and—

AMY G: And nothing happened.

SARAH: Since HR didn't do anything, what's the point of reporting? That doesn't just impact this particular situation; it impacts other situations. The trust between HR and employees is a real challenge when avoiding the conversation about trust issues is not going to make it better. You might as well put it out in the open where you admit it's kind of a black hole for a number of reasons. Often it's due to legal protection for the company. But there's much more we can do as individual employees, as managers, as team leaders to help create accountability around behavior and relationships on our own teams.

NICOLE: If you were one of those women who had reported and then saw that nothing had changed or happened, would you advise going to your manager or HR and asking for more information?

SARAH: Absolutely. If you wanted to have a better understanding of what was happening, you could ask. You might not get an answer, and that would feel frustrating. You could ask why they wouldn't give you the information. You could ask what to do in the future. Think about what you could be documenting. In that situation, if I was the person who reported, I would walk away feeling like I didn't trust HR or my company.

AMY G: As an HR manager, does regularly engaging in conversations about sexual harassment signal to people that it's something you care about?

SARAH: Yes. For example, if there were four HR managers at your company picnic and one of them is wearing a T-shirt from the last Rape Crisis Center gala and three are wearing sports T-shirts, which one are you going to feel the most comfortable reporting to? HR and managers should also think about supporting survivors of sexual abuse and assault. When you think about how many people will come into your workplace already having experienced some kind of sexual abuse or assault, that's an easy way to align yourself with the belief that this is not a place where you want people to be suffering in this way.

AMY B: You mentioned the whisper network. Say you hear something about a guy in the office. What's the right thing to do? Do you pass along the whisper?

SARAH: When I'm the recipient of the rumor, I'm always curious to know if this was something the person experienced directly. In which case, it's not a whisper network; it's a disclosure conversation. I would approach that differently. But if it's "I heard about that person doing something," I would not pass that information along. I might tell the guy's friend, but I am somebody who doesn't hesitate to speak up because of my background and experience. It is a privilege for me to feel that way. But I would say, "Listen, I know you're friends with this person. They have a reputation for being somebody that women don't want to work with. If you care about them, then you might want to talk to them about it."

AMY G: How does that guy then go talk to the person who's supposedly the harasser? What does he say?

SARAH: There's no one thing that the friend can say, and it will probably go badly. Hey, I've noticed you're kind of touchy feely with your colleagues. Have you thought about that, just in the context of #MeToo? This is why it's good to do training. The person might get mad but getting feedback on their behavior is important and critical. A lot of people don't feel confident enough to give that feedback.

If we can't even imagine ourselves having these kinds of conversations, we can't imagine the world changing. So, we're going to practice them and we're going to mess them up a few times. I've given feedback to somebody where I said, "I'm concerned about you. I care about you. I'm wondering about this interaction that you're having." The conversation didn't blow up. But sometimes these conversations don't go well, and what I try to tell myself in those moments is that the land mine was already there. I didn't want it to go off in my face, but it did. Those tensions exist and the behavior happens. I didn't create them, and I didn't create them by speaking up about them. They were already there, and I made sure that it didn't blow up on somebody who was more vulnerable than me.

AMY G: Often, especially for women who speak up, managers and sometimes HR have retaliated. How do you deal with that? How do you know if that's going to happen to you before you decide whether to speak up?

SARAH: If we are expecting the people with the least amount of power to be the ones who speak up, then of course there's going to be retaliation. Part of it is just creating power in numbers. But I think retaliation is real, so I'm very clear that if you choose not to report, that is a valid choice, one that absolutely makes sense given everything that we know about not just the formal retaliation, but the social retaliation. Or if you are somebody who maybe experienced sexual abuse or sexual assault and are emotionally retriggered by an unsafe work environment, do what you have to do to take care of yourself. Whatever choice you make is right. In the meantime, let's try to empower some more people who can speak up and intervene in the culture so that we don't have to continue to face incidents like this, where reporting causes retaliation.

AMY G: If you are a leader in an organization that's interested in having these proactive discussions, but you bring it up and you get blank stares or pushback, how can you make progress?

SARAH: Recognize that you need a series of conversations and ways of bringing people along. Most sexual harassment training is an internal communication strategy. If you put yourself in charge of the internal communication strategy for sexual harassment prevention and response, then think about your peers and how to help them understand the risks, including the risks to productivity. If an organization doesn't have psychological safety, it's not going to be productive. Some financial and legal risks are associated with this topic that an organization should really understand. It has serious reputational risks. At any point, somebody could complain about the organization in a very public way. And that would be much more expensive than investing in more training on the topic.

If you are overseeing a team and have a budget, you don't need to wait for HR to come up with online compliance training that's mandatory for everybody. You can start doing some of your own work around conflict and feedback, and bystander intervention. It's less about finding the perfect one and more about creating a series of conversations to allow the larger conversation to continue. To practice some of these scenarios and to talk through the different issues around both prevention and response at a team level. You don't have to wait for your CEO or HR to get on board to make a difference.

Nicole and the Amys continued the conversation after our guest signed off.

NICOLE: I'm still wondering about how to alleviate concerns about whether you're seeing something or when you're not sure what you're seeing?

AMY B: If you're not sure, don't come in hot. Don't come in with, "Hey, leave her alone." Maybe say, "Mary, great to see you. I wanted to talk to you about that meeting today." And just see what happens then.

AMY G: To Sarah's point, you have multiple choices: Do you intervene right now? Do you say something afterward? Do you go to HR? I get consumed with what's the right thing to do. Sometimes you just do something, and it may not be the right thing, and you may look back on it five years later and think you could have handled that differently. The conversation may blow up. The problem is that the decision becomes paralyzing.

At an off-site for a previous company I worked for, there was lots of alcohol involved. It was a big party, and I saw two people intensely involved in a conversation. The man kept touching the woman. In that situation, I thought that she wanted to be in the conversation, but he was someone with authority over her. A lot of people were whispering about it. None of us ever did anything. As far as I know nothing ever came of it, but looking back, why didn't I just go say, "Hey, do you guys want to dance?" Why didn't I intervene just in case something was going on? It's a hard thing to do.

AMY B: If the two people in the office whom Sarah mentioned wanted to be in that situation, the last thing you want to do is say, "Hey, I saw you guys leaning over the desk together." On the other hand, maybe the thing to do in that situation is to say to whoever you're closer to, "Um, the door was open when you guys were in there." There are no easy answers.

AMY G: Don't presume you know, but just ask questions or even say, "Hey, the door was open" and just give the person the opportunity to clarify or to ask for help or say that they wanted to be there. One of the things that worries me about the dynamics is that sometimes people feel like they need to be 100% sure that something happened before they say anything. That just reinforces the silence of victims, and even the silence of bystanders. It's not going to be 100% crystal clear what's happened or who perpetrated, or who's the victim. And we still need to talk about it.

AMY B: If you're the less powerful person in the scenario, you may not even realize something is going on. If you've ever been in this situation, you can be incredulous. You're asking yourself, what just happened here?

AMY G: I must have misunderstood them.

AMY B: Or, did what I think happened just happen?

AMY G: Right after #MeToo, one of our colleagues asked me if this was personal for me. I said no and then I listed five things that had happened. I just hadn't thought about them that way. There was the boss who asked me out. There was a client who was funny; I always loved being in meetings with him. Once he showed me a really inappropriate image on his computer. I just pretended it didn't happen so I could still have fun with him. We continued to have a good relationship. It was much easier for me to ignore it than to do something about it. Women make that calculation all the time.

NICOLE: You might not even think of that as sexual harassment. It could just be embarrassing. Someone said a really weird thing. It's awkward and uncomfortable, but we're going to ignore it to save face for everyone. Taken to an extreme, that could be really dangerous. But that happens on a smaller scale a lot of the time.

AMY G: What we learned from the research we published from the past few years is that those offenses unfortunately do add up, and they create an environment that allows more serious offenses.

Adapted from "Why Things Aren't Better, Yet," Women at Work *podcast, season 3, episode 9, June 10, 2019.*

10

Ending Harassment at Work Requires an Intersectional Approach

by Pooja Jain-Link, Trudy Bourgeois, and Julia Taylor Kennedy

If your company approaches the problem of sexual misconduct with one-size-fits-all solutions, chances are high you aren't protecting some of the most vulnerable members of your workforce. The experiences of women of color—and of men of color—are at risk of being misunderstood and undervalued.

In the Center for Talent Innovation's study "What #MeToo Means for Corporate America," we uncovered a nuanced, at times surprising, portrait of sexual misconduct.[1] Our research illustrates the varied landscapes professionals of different backgrounds face when it comes to sexual misconduct. It reveals the ways race and gender intersect to complicate our standard narrative of motive, and our standard image of a senior male perpetrator and junior female victim.[2]

After all, sexual harassment is not simply about sex. It is often a tool wielded to assert power and dominance. As Teresa Fitzsimmons, director of workplace dynamics at Lausanne Business Solutions, notes, "Sexual harassment is a signal of an individual having a lack of respect for another . . . [it] evolves out of disrespect and asymmetric power."[3] That asymmetric power can refer to men harassing women, but as we discovered in our research, race and seniority can complicate the picture.

Overall, we found that 34% of female employees have been sexually harassed by a colleague. When we broke down that number by race and job level, a more complex story began to emerge.

Among the Asian women we surveyed who had been harassed, nearly one in three (31%) say that the perpetrator was a junior colleague. This finding contradicts the common assumption that harassment only comes from above. The fact that so many women in this group report bottom-up harassment may stem from stereotypes that Asian women are deferential, easy targets for younger colleagues looking to assert power.[4] "There is the fetishization of Asian women that I see with a lot of white men," Mila, a Vietnamese American business development executive told us. "They expect us to be docile, easy, and exotic. But I hadn't expected that to carry over at work."

Similarly, nearly one in four Black women who have been sexually harassed say that the perpetrator was a more junior colleague (22%) or that the perpetrator was another woman (23%).

This same dynamic plays out vividly in our exploration of male victims of sexual misconduct. Men, we find, experience a deeper shame because of gender expectations. Misconduct compromises their masculinity, making it difficult to talk about incidents of harassment or assault.

Black men are far more likely to have been sexually harassed by a colleague than men of other backgrounds. More than one in five Black men have been sexually harassed by a colleague, compared to 13% of white men. And 85% of Black male victims have been harassed by a woman. Colleagues may be using harassment as a weapon to assert racial dominance; and the disproportionate harassment of Black men could stem from the historical fetishization of the Black male body, and Black men's dual legacy of being both feared and desired.[5]

Fortunately, there are solutions—solutions that take into account the need to report both above and below an employee's rank in the corporate hierarchy, dig into the unique dynamic of race, and engage the full workforce in the fight against sexual misconduct. Here are methods to consider.

Conduct a culture audit

Before a company implements solutions, it must try to understand the specific landscape of sexual misconduct at the organization. Are the perpetrators in your organization most likely to leverage the power status of their seniority, their gender, their race, or a combination of these factors? How do different cohorts experience sexual misconduct, and what solutions would be most effective in addressing the challenges of each group? Because of the sensitive nature of the topic, companies must commit to gathering the information anonymously if they want honest feedback. A culture audit has the added benefit of signaling to employees that management cares about the well-being of all employees. At Nike, an informal climate survey that demonstrated widespread perceptions of bias and misconduct at the company led to the ouster of several top executives and a strategy to improve the company's climate for women.[6]

Allow for truly confidential reporting

Innovative technology can make reporting sexual misconduct both a more transparent and a securely confidential process. Callisto is a platform that allows victims to log encrypted, time-stamped accounts of assault, with the option to surface the account to authorities if and only if someone else accuses the same person. The program was created in 2015 for use on college campuses but has recently spread to the professional workplace with Callisto Expansion. Callisto's approach ensures victims will not be a sole accuser and avoids "he said/she said" scenarios. It also empowers victims of color who are more likely to feel that their account would be ignored, or those whose account subverts our traditional understanding of sexual power dynamics, such as male victims of sexual misconduct.

Update your training

Cutting-edge training related to sexual misconduct and gender discrimination equips the full workforce to support victims and speak up against perpetrators. Consider creative approaches to training sessions, such as bystander training, civility norms and conversations, and opportunities for male allyship. Jackson Katz, founder and director of MVP Strategies, centers his trainings around toxic masculinity and teaches men at college campuses, locker rooms, and corporate offices across the country how to be allies. These types of trainings engage men and educate employees across all levels of the organization on the nuances of sexual misconduct, empowering them to speak up when they witness—or experience—behavior they may not have previously recognized as inappropriate or previously felt would not have been taken seriously.

Employers and individuals who seek to simplify the problem of sexual misconduct by ignoring the intersecting factors of race, gender, and seniority will succeed only in silencing and sidelining the historically disadvantaged. The best way we can all support the #MeToo movement as it marches on is by understanding the nuanced narrative, by challenging too-simple definitions of sexual misconduct and how it occurs, and by working to prevent all misconduct across gender, race, and hierarchy.

Adapted from content posted on hbr.org, April 23, 2019 (product # H04WSG).

SECTION THREE

Speak Out Against Racism

11

How to Call Out Racial Injustice at Work

by James R. Detert and Laura Morgan Roberts

In this time of intense pain, anger, and collective attention, many people—African Americans especially—are seizing the moment to speak truth to power at work. They are holding senior leaders accountable for their commitments to increased diversity; confronting colleagues or clients who make insensitive or ignorant comments; and calling out those who mock the Black Lives Matter movement or dismiss calls for justice and human rights.

Speaking up in this way is risky, but studies beyond the realm of conversations about race have shown that it is also vitally important. It's key to our individual and collective well-being, learning, and ultimately organizational performance.[1]

We desperately need people to be courageous enough to undertake these actions. So how can you take a stand for advancing racial justice in your own organization in a way that improves your chances for leading change from within, mitigates risk of rejection, and preserves your career options and mental health?

Speaking up about hard truths at work is difficult for just about everyone, especially about issues that in some way implicate those above us. We fear—for good reason—that we'll suffer career, social, psychological, or other kinds of harm for being honest about difficult issues.[2] When those issues directly implicate people's integrity, the risks of an in-the-moment explosion or after-the-fact consequences only escalate. Thus, people who champion diversity face a host of negative consequences because of widespread resistance toward targeted efforts to promote equity and inclusion.

As high as these stakes are for white people who speak up, they're higher if you're Black. Raise these issues and you risk being seen as biased, overly emotional (for example, too angry), and a host of other negative stereotypes that lie beyond the problems you're trying to get addressed.[3] Here's an insidious example from one of us (Jim): In one of my classes I present students with a story of a Black manager being called a racial slur by a white subordinate and ask what the Black boss should do. Students typically advise that the manager should turn to

HR for help so he won't be seen as unfair in his discipline of a white subordinate. Asked what they would tell the manager if he were white, some of those same students typically see him as capable of taking disciplinary action against a subordinate of any race without help.

Courageous actions are rooted in people's willingness to sacrifice their security and stability for the sake of a cause that is greater than their career advancement. But that doesn't mean that you should be cavalier about raising issues of racial justice. Our research has shown that there are ways to approach this work that mitigate your risk of being derailed or dismissed—and give you the best chance of being heard. Here are five strategies to help you maximize the impact of your courageous acts when speaking truth to power at work.

Use allies and speak as a collective

Find like-minded colleagues and raise the issue together. People we studied reported that speaking up as a group on workplace issues had more of an impact because it was hard to write them off as "one disgruntled person." Collective voice is especially impactful when it comes from a multicultural coalition of allies. It's harder to dismiss non-Black allies on the grounds of being biased or self-interested, and a unified voice shows that Black issues are *human*. If you can't find a group within your company, use social proof by pointing to others (ideally whose view the person you're speaking to respects or cares about) who share your point of view.

Channel your emotions (but don't suppress them)

Revealing the full extent of your rage or despair in front of those with power sets you up to be dismissed or punished for being "too emotional." It's completely normal to be angry (outraged!), hurt, and sad about the things we've witnessed time and again. (We are too!) And you shouldn't ignore these emotions: find safe spaces to help you to honor them so that you can channel them as energy that fuels your next steps—conversations with confidantes, for example, or with counselors. Then, after you are feeling centered, you might call attention to the racial injustice that occurred.

Here's an example. Terrence, a young Black man, confronted his significantly older, white boss about using racial slurs at work. It was a bold move for Terrence to call out this behavior in public given the hierarchical nature of the place and the knowledge that there were "a lot of racist people working there in higher positions." Despite the strong emotions he felt, Terrence spoke in a firm and measured way, showing compassion and a desire to help correct rather than shame or scold his boss. This allowed his boss to see the ignorance and hurtfulness of his statements and, according to one of Terrence's colleagues, led him to change his ways, rather than reacting defensively.

Anticipate others' negative reactions

As much as this feels like a time to focus on your own feelings of outrage and pain, you should also anticipate strong emotional reactions from the people you're confronting. Demanding improvements in racial equity stands a good chance of evoking defensiveness and fear. Inquiry and framing can help to defuse negative reactions and align shared goals.

For example, if your request evokes a furrowed brow or a crossing of arms across the chest, start asking questions: "These seem like appropriate next steps to me, but perhaps they feel problematic to you. Can you help me understand what you're thinking, and why these may not seem right to you?" You don't have to agree with what gets said next, but your effort to acknowledge that your counterpart has feelings too can increase your chance of reaching a mutually satisfactory outcome.

Frame what you say so that it's compelling to your counterpart

Delivering your message as inclusively as possible can help with the sense of divisiveness often associated with calls for racial justice. Make it easier for those you're imploring to change to see your message as coming from a position of "We are evolving together" rather than "I am revolting against you." This framing highlights collective progress, which—even when modest—helps people to cultivate positive identities and to find meaning and persistence in challenging projects at work.[4] If possible, make note of at least one way your organization has already made progress on racial inclusion (such as a town hall Q&A, public statement, task forces, investing in minority business enterprises) and try to build from there.

When you're trying to compel others to act differently, especially those above you, it's also critical to use language that will resonate with them, rather than the arguments that are meaningful only to you. Because of this, we often advocate leading with the economic or instrumental reasons for a change you're suggesting. However, in this case that's not a tenable option. Arguing for racial equity on the sole basis of financial gain suggests that basic justice and decency toward people of all races is optional unless it can be proven to have some economic advantage.[5] It's not, and it's yet another injury to people of color to require them to justify their demands for basic human rights in this degrading manner.

You can reframe this moral imperative in a way that resonates with your audience, however. If, for example, your boss is motivated by external threats, explain how your proposals will keep customers who are disgusted by your company's lack of action from abandoning you.

If your boss is more excited by opportunities, talk about how embracing this moral imperative will attract customers and top talent.

Follow up

After a difficult conversation, often the last thing we want to do is go engage the same people again anytime soon. But no matter how well you handled yourself in the first encounter, these topics are so sensitive that there's a decent chance someone you talked to left the discussion feeling personally indicted or that you felt misunderstood. If you need those people to stand with you for real change to take root, you'll want to check in.

Start by acknowledging the difficulty of the subject: "I know our conversation was a really tough one, and I imagine it could have left you with lingering feelings. Can we talk about that?" That can be a powerful way to move forward together and also gives you the opportunity to clarify misunderstandings and to nail down details like resource commitments, action steps, and agreements on measurement and accountability that can give your call for change a better chance of real success.

A final thought about the courage it takes to speak up in the workplace about racial injustice: If you have attempted to implement these suggestions and still see little to no progress, take stock of where you are and where you wish to be. It might be time to look around your organization for a new team or assignment with leaders and allies who are willing to join you in this work. Or, it might be time for you to find a new organization where you employ your talents among those more demonstrably committed to the changes you seek.

Adapted from content posted on hbr.org, July 16, 2020 (product #H05QRG).

12

When and How to Respond to Microaggressions

by Ella F. Washington, Alison Hall Birch, and Laura Morgan Roberts

Around the world, people are finally engaging in real conversations about race, justice, diversity, equality, and inclusion. That's a good thing, hopefully paving the way for meaningful antiracist action from both individuals and organizations. But those discussions will, in all likelihood, be very uncomfortable—not just for white employees and leaders who might be confronting their privilege for the first time but also for people of color, who know that candid talks with colleagues will mean they either face or need to call out "microaggressions."

What Microaggressions Look Like

Microaggressions are incidents in which someone accidentally (or purposely) makes an offensive statement or asks an insensitive question. They are defined as verbal, behavioral, and environmental indignities that communicate hostile, derogatory, or negative racial slights and insults to the target person or group.[1] For Black people, they are ubiquitous across daily work and life.

Here are a few seemingly innocuous statements that, in the context of racist assumptions and stereotypes, can be quite damaging.

> "When I see you, I don't see color" (signaling that the person doesn't acknowledge your Blackness or won't hold it against you).
>
> "We are all one race: the human race" (signaling that your experience as a Black person is no different from the experience of people of other races).
>
> "You are so articulate" (signaling that Black people are not usually capable of competent intellectual conversation).
>
> "I see your hair is big today! Are you planning to wear it like that to the client meeting?" (signaling that natural Black hairstyles are not professional).

"Everyone can succeed in society if they work hard enough" (signaling that disparate outcomes for Black people result from laziness).

As suggested by the name, microaggressions seem small, but compounded over time, they can have a deleterious impact on an employee's experience, physical health, and psychological well-being. In fact, research suggests that subtle forms of interpersonal discrimination like microaggressions are *at least as harmful* as more-overt expressions of discrimination.[2]

How to Respond to Microaggressions

Microaggressions reinforce white privilege and undermine a culture of inclusion. The best solution is, of course, increasing awareness of microaggressions, insisting that non-Black employees stop committing them, and calling out those who do. But in the absence of those changes—and understanding that complete prevention is probably impossible—how should Black employees and managers respond to the microaggressions they face, within and outside of current discussions around race in the workplace?

There are three main ways to react:

Let it go. For a long time, the most common default response was choosing not to address offensive comments in the workplace. Because they are pervasive yet subtle, they can be emotionally draining to confront. Yet silence places an emotional tax on Black employees, who are left wondering what happened and why, questioning their right to feel offended, and reinforcing beliefs that they are not safe from identity devaluation at work.[3]

Respond immediately. This approach allows the transgression to be called out and its impact explained while the details of the incident are fresh in the minds of everyone involved. Immediacy is an important component of correcting bad behavior. But this approach can be risky. The perpetrator might get defensive, leaving the target feeling as if they somehow "lost control," did not show up as their best self, and will be labeled an overly sensitive whiner, a troublemaker, or the stereotypical angry Black person.[4]

Respond later. A more tempered response is to address the perpetrator privately at a later time to explain why the microaggression was offensive. Here, the risk lies in the time lag. A follow-up conversation requires helping the person who committed the microaggression to first recall it and then to appreciate its impact. The Black employee bringing it up might be deemed petty—like someone who has been harboring resentment or holding on to "little things" while the other party, having "meant no harm," has moved on. Such accusations are a form of racial gaslighting, which can be very damaging.[5]

We recommend the following framework for determining which course is best for you in any given situation and then, if you decide to respond, ensuring an effective dialogue.

Discern

Determine how much of an investment you want to make in addressing the microaggression. Do not feel pressured to respond to every incident; rather, feel empowered to do so when you decide you should. Consider:

- **The importance of the issue and the relationship.** If either is or both are important to you, avoidance is the wrong approach.[6] Express yourself in a way that honors your care for the other party, and assert yourself in a way that acknowledges your concern about the issue.
- **Your feelings.** Microaggressions can make you doubt the legitimacy of your reactions. Allow yourself to feel what you feel, whether it's anger, disappointment, frustration, aggravation, confusion, embarrassment, exhaustion, or something else. Any emotion is legitimate and should factor into your decision about whether, how, and when to respond. With more-active negative emotions such as anger,

it's often best to address the incident later. If you're confused, an immediate response might be preferable. If you're simply exhausted from the weight of working while Black, maybe it is best to let it go—meaning best for you, not for the perpetrator.[7]

- **How you want to be perceived now and in the future.** There are consequences to speaking up and to remaining silent. Only you can determine which holds more weight for you in any specific situation.

Disarm

If you choose to confront a microaggression, be prepared to disarm the person who committed it. One reason we avoid conversations about race is that they make people defensive. Perpetrators of microaggressions typically fear being perceived—or worse, revealed—as racist.[8] Explain that the conversation might get uncomfortable for them but that what they just said or did was uncomfortable for you. Invite them to sit alongside you in the awkwardness of their words or deeds while you get to the root of their behavior together.

Defy

Challenge the perpetrator to clarify their statement or action. Use a probing question, such as "How do you mean that?" This gives people a chance to check themselves as they unpack what happened. And it gives you an opportunity to better gauge the perpetrator's intent. One of the greatest privileges is the freedom not to notice you have privilege, so microaggressions are often inadvertently offensive. Acknowledge that you accept their intentions to be as they stated but reframe the conversation around the impact of the microaggression.[9] Explain how you initially interpreted it and why. If they continue to assert that they "didn't mean it like that," remind them that you appreciate their willingness to clarify their intent and hope they appreciate your willingness to clarify their impact.

Decide

You control what this incident will mean for your life and your work—what you will take from the interaction and what you will allow it to take from you. Black people, as well as those with various other marginalized and intersectional identities, are already subject to biased expectations and evaluations in the workplace.[10] Life is sufficiently taxing without allowing microaggressions to bring you down.[11] Let protecting your joy be your greatest and most persistent act of resistance.[12]

A Note to Non-Black Allies

A note of advice for non-Black allies old and new: The work of allyship is difficult. You will make mistakes as you learn—and you will always be learning. For anyone accused of committing a microaggression or counseling someone who has been accused, here are a few notes on how to respond:

- Remember that intent does not supersede impact.
- Seek to understand the experiences of your Black peers, bosses, and employees without making them responsible for your edification.
- Believe your Black colleagues when they choose to share their insights; don't get defensive or play devil's advocate.
- Get comfortable rethinking much of what you thought to be true about the world and your workplace and accept that you have likely been complicit in producing inequity.

Although more organizations are encouraging candid discussions on race in the workplace, we cannot ignore the historical backlash that Black employees have endured for speaking up. Cultural change takes time and intention. So while we encourage timely and strategic dialogue about microaggressions, it is ultimately up to each individual to respond in the way that is most authentic to who they are and how they want to be perceived.

Adapted from content posted on hbr.org, July 3, 2020 (product #H05Q4G).

13

How to Disrupt a System That Was Built to Hold You Back

by Lan Nguyen Chaplin

I've been working in academia for two decades. My colleagues would probably describe me as someone with "an upbeat personality" who's obsessed with learning and being a good peer. I might even describe myself, or the side of me that shows up for work every day, in the same way.

But there is another side, a more private one, that lives in me too. I'm an Asian American woman who has fought her way into the position of tenured professor. I'm the daughter of Vietnamese refugees who came to the United States to build a better life. I'm the youngest of 14 children and the mother of two. And while I consider my background one of many blessings and am grateful for the doors that have opened for me, I've also faced a great deal of racism and sexism throughout my career as a result of who I am and where I come from.

When I taught my first MBA class of nearly 60 students, whispers infiltrated the room the moment I walked up to the podium. A student yelled out, "How long have you been teaching?"

Their question, however jarring, was unsurprising. I'm petite and have often been told that I "look and sound" young. When people think about what a successful professor, or leader, looks like, they usually think of a white man: Women represent only 22% of full professors in business schools, or those employed at the highest rank.[1] Only 3% of full professors are female and Asian in all of academia.[2]

In this instance, I turned to my student and said what I always say: "I'm a lot younger than I look."

The room, as if on cue, erupted in laughter.

Like many women in my position, I've become savvy at responding to these kinds of comments and occurrences. You observe things from a special vantage point when you live in a world and work in an industry that was built to hold you back. The perspective, blind spots, and biases of people who have never questioned their right to take up space or fought to be heard becomes obvious. If you're a woman, more specifically, a woman of color in a predominantly white field, you already know that.

Whether you work in academia or not, whether you are seasoned or just beginning your career, there are going to be times when you enter a space that doesn't welcome you with open arms. In almost every industry, women of color receive less support and experience double standards, microaggressions, and unconscious bias, making it much more difficult to advance our careers in rank and pay.

This kind of discrimination needs to be addressed at the institutional, organizational, and leadership levels. It is their problem to solve, and not ours. Nonetheless, when you are trying to excel inside of these environments, it's a lot to go up against.

I want to share with you a handful of tools I've developed over the years to protect myself, my career path, and my mental health in an industry that I was never meant to succeed in. Take the ones that feel right for you and use them to disrupt the system that is getting in your way.

Allyship

The most important lesson I've learned over the years: There is power in numbers, and this is true at every level of an institution.

People tend to favor those who look like them, meaning those in positions of power tend to look, sound, and think in similar ways.[3] It's harder for women of color, in general, to establish networks that can help them navigate their careers in predominantly white industries.

As an Asian American woman, the "model minority" myth made this difficult for me in my early career. I came from a low-income family with limited economic resources and a lack of social networks, and yet I was expected to excel with little structural support. The myth not only erases the individual struggles Asian Americans face, but also ignores the role racism plays in the struggles of other racial or ethnic groups, and worse, it pits people of color against each other when we should really be allies.

To create any kind of change, in any industry, our voices need to be heard. The more voices there are, the louder we will be. This knowledge is your secret sauce: use it to connect with people in your office or at your institution who may feel disconnected and overlooked themselves.

Your ally can be an inclusive leader who wants to confront bad behavior and overturn patterns of injustice at the top. This person can create forward momentum for you by drawing attention to your contributions and recommending you for opportunities that advance your career. You can find them by asking around ("What's it like to work with . . . ?"). If they are worth connecting with, they will appreciate your initiative, and reply to your email—if you keep it short and to the point.

Your ally can also be someone at your rank who will put in the work to listen to you, understand you, learn from you, share their own story, and act on what they've learned. This is the person in the room who you hold in high esteem and, importantly, who holds you in high esteem as well. Take their support and keep paying it forward. Expand your network of allies and continue to support people from other marginalized groups.

Confrontation

When people make assumptions based on my appearance, I don't assume they are hurting me on purpose, but the pain is palpable. Every year, I watch people act on their implicit biases to judge my character, abilities, and potential. Well-intentioned staff comment, "You're such a cute China doll," "You're exotic. You've got big eyes for an Asian." Well-intentioned students swear, "You don't look like a professor" and "I thought you were one of us." Well-intentioned people ask, "Where are you *really* from?" All believe that their words are compliments.

But are they?

No matter how conscious, unconscious, or seemingly kind a bias is, it has the same outcome: inequality, exclusion, and reopened wounds. In my case, not being viewed as a professor translates to not being respected as a leader or deserving of my rank. Not being viewed as an American translates to not belonging—a feeling I have been battling since childhood.

When I was a kid, I was only allowed to speak to my parents in their first language. They raised me to take pride in our heritage, but at home, I still struggled to feel like I was Vietnamese. Morning kindergarten class and afternoon *Mister Rogers* taught me English and U.S. culture, but at school, I still struggled to feel like a "real American."

So you see, even though the issue lies at the institutional level, it's personal. For my own mental health, for my survival and growth, I've had to get comfortable confronting these biases when they *confront me*. Because it's what I can control. Because its effective. Because I need to set boundaries to focus on what matters: my work.

This was not easy to do when I was just starting out, but the more I practiced, the better I got.

Here's a (very) quick take on what I've learned about confronting biases:

- Schedule a private one-on-one meeting. Conversations that take place at the same eye level in a neutral space are most respectful and, therefore, helpful.

- Focus on the other person's *behaviors*. This will remind you that, more often than not, there are bad behaviors, not bad people. People grow and change. People have bad days. People say things without listening to what they actually said. Approach them with an interest in nurturing the professional relationship.

- Speak in a matter-of-fact tone. You want your message to take center stage, not your emotions. Avoid blaming, labeling, yelling, swearing, sarcasm, insults, or threats. Avoid inaccurate overgeneralizations, like "always," "never," "everything," and "nothing."

- Don't bring up past events that could be misconstrued as a personal attack and derail the conversation. Focus the conversation on a single incident. This will help the other person gain insight into what happened and why it was wrong, whereas bringing up multiple incidents at once may feel overwhelming and cause the other person to shut down entirely.

- When discussing the incident, make sure you can articulate and support your point with evidence.

- If the conversation gets heated, suggest a coffee break and reconnect in 10 minutes.

- Really *listen* to what the other person says when they respond. Have the intent of understanding where they are coming from. I find that asking questions helps clarify ("Can you please help me better understand . . . ?" "What did you mean by . . . ?")

- End the meeting by thanking the other person for taking the time to engage and listen ("I'm glad you understand that . . . and you'll work to . . . I now understand better . . ."). Ending the meeting this way nurtures the relationship.

Disruption

Pain usually accompanies growth. The biggest milestones in your young adulthood—moving away from home, going to college, finding your first job, and so on—are going to come with challenges that are unique to you and your situation. People of color often face additional challenges because we have fewer resources to support us. Today, a big part of my job in academia is doing just that: supporting and mentoring students of color.

I love and value this work, but I have also been punished for it throughout my career. Women are regularly stereotyped as being nice, compassionate, and warm. These positive traits supposedly make us good caretakers, but not powerful, competitive, and competent leaders.[4] In academia, women of color are tasked with the emotional labor of mentoring students who feel marginalized, and women in general do more committee work than men, which can decrease our research productivity and our chances of getting promoted.[5]

If you are also tasked with the emotional labor of mentoring others, thank you! Your work is needed, especially right now. However, if this work is going unrecognized and decreasing your productivity in areas that are recognized, you need to either stop saying yes to service or begin to work collaboratively with top leaders at your organization to build service into your reward model. Everyone in every industry, but especially in higher education, needs to be discussing how to create more diverse, equitable, and inclusive environments. Your service is a part of advancing that mission, meaning you should be rewarded equally—and you can and should be a part of this conversation.

Turn to your allies. Together, reach out to people in positions of power at your organization or institution who have publicly shared their commitment to diversity, equity, and inclusion (DEI). A part of disrupting the system is not just asking these leaders to include you in their conversations, but also inviting them into the conversations you are having around what needs to change.

Remember that you need *their help* to create that change, and they need *your help* to align their commitment to DEI with your institution's mission and values.

Final Thought

If your experience is anything like mine, you may have been expected to quietly "go along" for most of your life, and now your career. The hidden message here is that people may want you to be nonconfrontational, easy to work with, and docile—a stereotype that is especially common for women of Asian descent. It took time, but today, when I speak up or do things differently than what is expected of me, whether by students or other professors, I make no apologies.

Sure, I'm still perceived as difficult, out for herself, and bossy sometimes. But—and you need to hear this sooner than later—the expectation that you should agree with a point you don't support or go along with an idea without asking "how" or "why" is absurd.

We should never forget that it is ultimately the responsibility of the institution and the organization to address these inequalities. Nevertheless, there is a silver lining for us, the individuals being affected. Although women of color, including myself, often struggle with feelings of acceptance in many industries, it is these same feelings that can ignite a fire in us. Use this fire to find purpose in your work, to find your allies, and to challenge the status quo—something most of us have been practicing our entire lives. And do these things for yourself, if and when they feel good.

You're powerful. You're worthy. You deserve to take up space and be heard.

Adapted from content posted on hbr.org, March 8, 2021.

14

Women of Color Get Asked to Do More "Office Housework." Here's How to Say No

by Ruchika Tulshyan

Selena Rezvani was in an all-day strategy session when she faced a challenge many women of color are intimately familiar with: She was expected to arrange lunch for everyone present.

Simultaneously, seven heads in the room turned toward her, the only nonwhite person in the room, to place the order. "No one seemed to consider asking the white guy next to me who was my [same] age and level," recalls Rezvani, now VP of consulting and research at Be Leaderly, and author of *Pushback*. "The silent agreement in the room was unnerving."

The Problem

The unwavering conviction that it was the duty of the woman of color to do less-important tasks around the office was a common situation among the women of color whom I interviewed for this story. One woman told me: "I'm often asked to shut the door in a meeting, even if I'm sitting far away from the door. I did it earlier in my career, but these days I just say no."

These aren't just anecdotal experiences. Research from the Center for WorkLife Law at the University of California, Hastings College of the Law, has shown that women and people of color often wind up with worse assignments than their white male counterparts, hindering their ability to be promoted. In their article about this research, Joan Williams and Marina Multhaup define "office housework" as everything from "administrative work that keeps things moving forward, like taking notes or finding a time everyone can meet" to "work that's important but undervalued, like initiating new processes or keeping track of contracts" and work that's "usually not tied to revenue goals, so [these efforts] are far less likely to result in a promotion than, say, chairing an innovation or digital transformation committee."[1]

Research shows that white women face challenges to advancement in every industry. However, the statistics for women of color are worse: We face a "double jeopardy," where we experience bias related to both our gender and our race.[2]

Shutting the door or ordering lunch doesn't take a lot of time, but doing these tasks negatively reinforces the power dynamics that place women of color in lower positions. And they're faced with two unappealing options. They can either do the task and risk being constantly expected to complete these tasks, which Williams and Multhaup's research has shown to impair their ability to get promoted. Or they can say no and risk being penalized.[3]

Caty, a manager at a technology company who requested I not share her last name, says, "As a visibly Black woman in the workplace, I am often caught in a double-bind where if I don't accept the office housework, I'm considered an 'Angry Black' woman."

The professional women of color I spoke with told me they've been characterized as aggressive, out of character, or too emotional when they advocate for themselves in the workplace. While all women walk a tightrope between being liked and respected, for women of color, the experience is particularly egregious.[4]

The Solution

The most obvious solution here is to change the culture of these organizations so people in power don't make these requests. But that takes time. And while I hesitate to put the onus on women to fix the problem, I want to offer tips to help women of color who find themselves in these situations, while we continue pushing leaders for equity.

Turn down office housework requests *without* being penalized, with this roundup of advice from successful women of color.

Have a watertight refusal in place

It's smart to have a solid argument ready. You might say, "I was hired to do *X* and doing *Y* would take away time from completing *X* well." For on-the-spot requests like ordering lunch, I've used, "I really need to be present during this discussion as it's critical to what I'm working on." For longer-term requests, like constantly being asked to lead mentoring activities (which research has shown is one of the time-consuming "organizational citizenship" tasks that women are asked to take on), I've said something like, "I'm working on [very important project], and I'm worried I won't have the bandwidth to be helpful to [said mentee]."[5]

Arm yourself with evidence

Most people make these kinds of requests without realizing the impact on women of color. Evidence can help them understand the cumulative effect. Olive Goh, a director in the financial industry, told me that a friend of hers made a list of revenue-generating tasks she was responsible for, as well as all the nonrevenue-generating expectations that were placed on her. She created similar lists for men at the same level in her organization and took those lists to her boss. This made it easier for her to decline the housework tasks or to at least make the case for splitting them more evenly with the men in her office.

Offer a "no" and a "communal give"

"Women face less backlash in negotiations when they make their request communal ('it benefits us') rather than personal ('it benefits me')," says Rezvani. She coaches her female clients to consider saying no to lower-prestige tasks—planning a meeting, for example—and then offering a yes to higher-caliber ones that would give their team an edge, like performing a competitor analysis.

Check with your manager

In previous jobs, I would regularly double-check with my managers if I was asked to take on nonessential work. Getting them to sign off on whether the task was necessary helped me better understand whether saying no would get me labeled as "difficult." Rezvani advises setting up expectations in advance with your manager. "Contract verbally with your manager that they will back you up and provide cover," she says. If your boss agrees that the task isn't necessary or worth your time, it's easier to avoid the backlash from saying no.

Ask for more information

You can ask the requester why they're specifically encouraging you to do this extra labor, says Caty. "Have them tell you what unique and/or specific traits make you best suited to do this work. This will help the requester think critically about why they requested you do the labor as opposed to others who are also capable."

Use humor

Acknowledge, with some levity, the absurdity of women doing more office work than men, says Rezvani. "You can say to a man: 'Research shows that I'm more likely to get asked to do this kind of thing than you, and that you're going to like me less when I decline. But guess what I'm going to do?'" I'm not humorous by nature, but making light of the situation has helped me in my own career. I once responded by saying, "I'd rather [male colleague] ordered lunch as I'm already in charge of meals at home," and then cracked a smile. Rezvani also heard one woman quip, "My answer is no, that is, if it's OK with you."

Rotate tasks

If you're on a team that meets regularly, propose that you all rotate tasks like facilitating, taking notes, scheduling, and so on, advises Rezvani. This sets the expectation from day one that everyone has equal value to contribute.

Practice saying no with allies

With practice, saying no will become easier. I've previously written about a group of female professors at Carnegie Mellon who formed an "I just can't say no" club to help them refuse what they called "office favors."[6] Cultivating this network of allies becomes particularly important for women of color as we progress. Enlist colleagues to help you figure out collectively how to refuse office housework requests in a manner that feels authentic to you.

If you can't say no, at least get credit for the work

Sometimes there's no way to decline the work. In those cases, find a way to acknowledge that this work is "extra labor," says Caty, especially in performance reviews and in conversations with your manager. You want people to understand that you're taking on extra responsibilities and not assume these chores are part of your job description. Caty advises, however: "If the labor continues to not be recognized or rewarded, I'd either stop doing the work or leave the team or organization."

Use your influence to break norms

As you climb the ranks, pay it forward. Rezvani says, "When someone suggests that the smart female manager you happen to mentor could do the booth setup at the expo, call out that it's below their pay grade: 'I don't think it's a good use of Camilla's technical experience and skills to deploy her that way.'"

There's growing evidence that women of color toe a narrower line between being respected and liked. It's imperative that leaders understand and work toward mitigating the impact of office housework on the careers of multicultural women. In the meantime, I encourage more women of color to say no to these requests.

Adapted from content posted on hbr.org, April 6, 2018 (product #H0496I).

SECTION FOUR

Men

Be Allies and Amplify Voices

15

How Men Can Confront Other Men About Sexist Behavior

by W. Brad Johnson and David G. Smith

Globally, most men support gender equality and believe they are contributing in meaningful ways.[1] While some men may be doing their part in interpersonal allyship—mentorships and other professional relationships and support to push women forward—few are helping with public allyship—becoming courageous watchdogs for equity, dignity, respect, and fairness in the workplace. Perhaps this explains evidence showing that 77% of men believe they are doing all they can to support gender equality, while only 41% of women agree.[2] That means men must do more to speak up and speak out when they see bad behavior.

Active confrontation of other men for sexism, bias, harassment, and all manner of inappropriate behavior may be the toughest part of male allyship. It is also utterly essential. For many men, challenging masculine workplace norms is where the cost of allyship gets real in a hurry. We define confrontation this way: bringing sexism and exclusion of women to the attention of men who knowingly or unknowingly instigate and perpetuate these attitudes and outcomes in their words and actions.

Why is it so important that men stand willing to confront other men when they demean, offend, or harass—even if it's unintentional? There are several reasons. First, women who call out bad male behavior often are evaluated negatively, even rated as less competent compared to a man that does the same.[3] Second, when a man (someone without an apparent vested interest in gender fairness and equity) confronts bias or sexism, observers are more likely to be persuaded.[4] Third, how a message is received is often less about precise wording and more about the in-group identity of the speaker.[5] A confrontation intended to change attitudes and behavior has more impact when it comes from someone perceived to be similar—in this case, another man who can claim, "That's not who we [men] are" and "That's not what we [guys] do." Finally, quite often, men fear they're the only guy in the room who objects to a sexist comment or raunchy joke (though evidence shows lots of men are offended), so they stay silent when they could break the spell and enable other male allies to find their voice if only they'd speak up.[6]

While the prospect of speaking up against transgressions can feel overwhelming, there are steps you can take to make it easier. Drawn from our research for our book *Good Guys*, here are six confrontation strategies you can apply right now in your interactions at work.

Use the two-second rule

The well-documented bystander effect too often plays out in the workplace when men stay on the sidelines, timid and mute in the face of obvious gender bias and sexism. To combat the paralysis that sets in mere seconds after another man delivers a sexist comment or demeaning joke, just say something! We recommend the ouch technique: Simply say "Ouch!" clearly and forcefully. This buys you a few extra seconds to formulate a clear statement about why the comment didn't land well with you. Then, have some ready responses cued up in advance, such as:

> "Did you really mean to say that?"
>
> "We don't do that here."
>
> "That wasn't funny."
>
> "Actually, that's an outdated stereotype."

When you say something, own it

When you confront another man, don't attribute your concern or offense to the fact that there's a woman in the room or that women might be offended. Too often we hear half-hearted confrontations such as, "Come on, Bob. There are women in the room." This implies that Bob's sexist comment would be acceptable if no women were in sight.

Instead, use clear I-statements to signal that the behavior didn't land the right way with you, such as, "I didn't find that joke amusing, Bob. I don't appreciate the way it demeans women," or "I'd really appreciate it if you'd stop referring to our female colleagues as 'girls.' They are women."

Use Socratic questions as a confrontation device

Quite often, a Socratic question can serve both to disrupt gender bias and to trigger self-reflection in a male colleague. For instance, many women have experienced having a creative idea ignored during a meeting, only to have it repackaged by a male before the meeting ends. Next time you bear witness to such co-opting of a female colleague's idea, ask a thoughtful question designed to remind everyone in the room—including the offender—who generated the idea in the first place: "I'm confused,

Charles. How is that any different from what Amber suggested a few minutes ago?" The Socratic question can also be quite effective in helping a male colleague consider an alternative perspective. Lisen Stromberg of Prismwork Consulting recommends something as simple as, "I wonder if you've considered that women might experience this differently?"

Share what you've learned through a personal experience or relationship

Sometimes, confrontation through self-disclosure can be a powerful approach. Sharing authentically how bias or sexism was harmful to someone close to you can cause other men to do a double take, seeing their own behavior through a new lens. Saying, calmly but firmly, "My wife experienced this at work, and it's unacceptable! I don't want women to experience that here," can be deeply influential for other men. You can even make this aspirational by connecting this feedback to who he wants to be by saying, "I know you're a good guy, and I wouldn't want you to inadvertently offend women by suggesting they should smile more."

Use humor now and then

Particularly when you have an existing relationship with a male coworker or peer, try a short humorous observation as an intervention. For instance, when a guy calls a female colleague "sweetheart," try, "Do you call all your software developers 'sweetheart'?" Or, when a team member regularly interrupts your female colleague in a meeting, try some sports-related humor. Toss a yellow sticky note on the table, and say, "Penalty! That's 10 yards for interrupting."

Show him that you're on his side

Creating real behavior change in other men is best achieved through an artful blend of challenge and reinforcement. A group of real allies can turn confrontation into "carefrontation" as one informal group of executive leaders shared with us. So, when a guy goes off the rails with sexism or harassing humor, first, use language that lets him know you see him as part of your tribe and that your heart is in the right place. Pull him aside after a meeting and have a direct conversation. Show that you are worried about him; use I-statements that aren't accusatory, but also let him know how you feel as a friend and colleague. In clarifying the precise behavior of concern, be specific in the details, situation, and people involved. You don't have to take the conversation to DEFCON 5, but you do have to make him understand how his behavior is hurting others, sabotaging his credibility, and why you care. Then, when he shows some gender awareness or an inclusive mindset, be sure to follow up with some positive reinforcement.

Confronting other men about their missteps is not about humiliation, shaming, or angry altercations. And there is no one-size-fits-all approach. At times, a private conversation after the meeting will get a more positive result, especially if the perpetrator is a close colleague, open to feedback, and well-meaning but naive, or out of step with changing attitudes and expectations. At other times it is essential to confront in public, especially if the comment or behavior was egregious and likely to dispirit coworkers and damage the relational environment, or if the perpetrator is a serial offender, rigid in his attitudes toward women, and unlikely to respond to private corrective feedback.

Allyship is hard work. It takes a deft touch and a thoughtful and empathetic ally to create lasting and meaningful change. Excellent allies have the courage to get comfortable doing the uncomfortable work of disrupting the status quo.

Adapted from content posted on hbr.org, October 16, 2020 (product #H05XQI).

16

How to Show White Men That Diversity and Inclusion Efforts Need Them

by Lily Zheng

Most leaders of big corporations outwardly support diversity and inclusion efforts. But in my work as a diversity and inclusion (D&I) consultant, I frequently get a behind-the-scenes look at how leaders truly feel, and a surprising number of people—from line managers to C-suite executives—express notedly less enthusiastic opinions in private.

"It seems like I'm not wanted in the room when D&I conversations start happening," one person told me. "It feels like I'm part of the problem," another said in frustration. And a third, in a rare admission of a common sentiment said, "It seems like everyone is out to get the white guys."

According to the White Men's Leadership Study, a study of white men and diversity and inclusion, the single biggest challenge to engaging in D&I efforts—as noted by almost 70% of white men surveyed—is knowing whether they are "wanted."[1] This may sound like an unfounded sentiment to D&I practitioners who make great efforts to involve leaders in their initiatives, but rather than dismiss this reluctance, it would be far better to understand how and why it happens. Understanding root causes will allow us to figure out how to make leaders into allies, not enemies.

Why Some Leaders Feel Defensive

Even innocuous comments that identify the existence of identity-based discrimination may land very differently with different people. For individuals who have experienced marginalization, these comments can feel empowering, giving voice to their experiences. Others may respond empathetically, even if they haven't had the specific experience referenced. But for some people, especially those who have never faced marginalization for their identities, these comments can land the wrong way. Why?

One of the functions of privilege is rarely having to think about privileged identities as "identities." In America, historical power inequities make it so women, people of color, religious minorities, disabled people, and LGBTQ+ people are constantly reminded of their differences, while men, white people, able-bodied people, straight people, and cisgender people can go their entire lives without thinking actively about their masculinity, whiteness, abled bodies, heterosexuality, or cisgender status. For privileged leaders, seemingly innocuous workplace comments can be some of the first times they explicitly think about their race, gender, or sexuality. These leaders may hear mentions of a group they belong in, find those parts of their identities more salient than ever, and sensing critique, get defensive.

Take these examples. When a woman says, "A man catcalled me the other day at work," a white man in the audience might sit up a little straighter, thinking consciously or subconsciously, *I'm a man, and my group is being attacked!* If someone asserts that "white fragility makes hard conversations about race even harder," a white person might think, *I'm white, and being characterized as "fragile" is offensive!* Or when a queer person admits, "My teammates hurt me when they assume I'm straight like them," their colleague might think, *I'm straight, is that supposed to be my fault?*

Sociologist Robin DiAngelo calls these sorts of defensive overreactions to race-based criticisms "white fragility," and argues that it stems from a lack of "racial stamina" due to white people's insulation from genuine conversations about race. They haven't had a safe space to explore these topics, and for many people, this is the first time they've thought carefully about their identity.

It's clear we all, especially D&I practitioners, need to offer psychologically safe spaces for white people and privileged people to explore these conversations. Otherwise, we will continue to encounter defensiveness and won't get the support we seek from these leaders. In my own work, I've found two practices that help: framing identity as insight and focusing on equality.

Framing Identity as Insight

D&I practitioners often frame identity as valuable, but only do so for marginalized identities. The rationale (which I agree with) is that uplifting people of color, women, LGBTQ+ people, immigrants, Jewish people, and so on is necessary to counter the marginalization they experience in society, and it doesn't make sense to uplift straight white men for whom society is built. But building a D&I initiative on this rationale contributes to feelings that straight white men don't belong, a cost we can't afford in companies where power lies in the hands of the privileged.

We can, however, reframe this rationale into a strengths-based approach: identity as insight.

Consider this statement: "White people have a powerful and partial understanding of how race works in society."

Statements like these name a privileged identity (white), attach constrained value to it (powerful and partial), and then situate it in a context that encourages future conversation (how race works in society). They are also easy to expand into larger conversations with questions like, "How do other racial groups understand how race works in society? How are their experiences different? Why?"

I used this framing recently with a group of leaders participating in an equitable and inclusive leadership class. "You're all experts in how gender works in your workplace." The women in the room nodded, but the men looked more dubious.

"I know a lot about how my *workplace* works," one man commented. "What to do if you want a promotion, how to resolve problems, how decisions get made. But my wife is teaching me that things don't work the same for her. She's the expert in gender, not me."

I reframed his first statement. "What you're saying is that your wife knows a lot about how your workplace works for women and that you know a lot about how your workplace works *for men.*"

Focusing on Equality

Equality or "fairness" is one of the most powerful shared beliefs in our culture: that everyone should have a fair shot at life and be rewarded for what they have achieved.

When working with straight white male leaders, I often tell them, "I know you care about equality in your organization. And being a straight white man gives you enormous insight and expertise into how your organization works for other people like you. It's your job as a leader to figure out what it's like for other people and make sure everyone has a positive experience." These three sentences help in several ways. First, they name the often unnamed identities of straight, white, and man without blame or shame. Second, they celebrate the value of these identities in the form of expertise, while also being honest about the limits of such expertise. (A straight white man will not, for example, start off knowing what their organization is like for a bisexual indigenous woman.) And third, they explicitly tie the humility and curiosity necessary for successful D&I work to what it means to be a good leader.

In the 1970s, Elliot Aronson and his students developed and popularized a teaching technique called the "Jigsaw Classroom" that involved giving each student in a group part of a solution and requiring they collaborate to solve a problem.[2] This is an interdependent act of shared learning, in which everyone brings valuable knowledge and no one person can come to an answer themselves and an apt analogy for how we can bring more privileged leaders into D&I efforts. By understanding our unique experiences as pieces of a complex puzzle, we can defuse defensiveness and find a way to together create a more equitable world.

Adapted from content posted on hbr.org, October 28, 2019 (product #H058DP).

17

Use Your Social Network as a Tool for Social Justice

by Raina Brands and Aneeta Rattan

Millions of individuals around the world are protesting in solidarity with the Black Lives Matter movement, and many are asking themselves how they can bring the same spirit of solidarity into their work lives. Or, as one of our colleagues recently expressed in an email: "I don't want to be one of those white males who is privately sympathetic. I want to actively champion women and minorities."

The good news is that majority group members and men have an immense source of power at their disposal to prevent and confront bias in the workplace: their social networks. Here's how to take action.

Broadcast Antiracist, Antisexist Values

You have a bigger sphere of influence than you realize. Most people think about their immediate circle of friends as their audience. However, research in the study of social networks has shown they are wrong.[1] Your ideas and behaviors ripple out from you, influencing your friends, friends of friends whom you may not even know, and friends of those friends as well. In fact, a whole range of outcomes are influenced by these third-order ties—your weight, your values and beliefs, even your risk of divorce.[2] This is your sphere of influence, in both your place of work and your daily life.

How can this help you contribute to an antiracist, antisexist workplace? The answer is deeply rooted in our psychology. We are a fundamentally social species.[3] From an evolutionary perspective, we survive not as individuals but rather because of our ability to get along with others and work as a group. This means that we experience a lot of emotional tension when we disagree with our friends on issues that are important to us. It also means that when new ideas and proposals are made in the workplace—such as diversity and inclusion initiatives—we are primed to adopt our friends' views of those initiatives in order to maintain an emotionally balanced state.

So if my friend likes the diversity and inclusion initiative, then I am more likely to support the diversity and inclusion initiative.

The implication is that you have enormous capacity to influence others to be antiracist and to be antisexist in the workplace—those you know directly and individuals as many as three social steps away from you. But to make a real impact, you must move your conversations with colleagues, and what you share online, beyond value statements toward concrete antibias actions. Share your support for debiasing your organization with your friends, engage them in conversations about the problems of bias and exclusion in your workplace, and tell them what actions you are taking to make your team fair and inclusive. Unless they are committed to racism and sexism, they will be influenced to share your sentiments, and to speak with their friends about it, who then will do the same.

How do you enact this, concretely? Take the example of a manager who talks over your Black team member at every meeting. Assuming you have noticed this, first touch base with your team member to both confirm that this is their experience and ask for permission to subtly intervene. (After all, they may face backlash from any type of confrontation.) If you are able to intervene—perhaps by pointing out that your colleague was not finished speaking and returning the floor to them—you can then discuss this interaction with both your work friends and your out-of-work friends. Those friends will then share aspects of that conversation with their friends, and so on.

Because of the power of the network, you want to be thoughtful about how you speak and what you share—the point of this is not to offer yet another trite and untrue white male savior narrative. Every detail will not make it through the network, so you must highlight the right ones: You have started to notice subtle biases in your own workplace, you are bothered by them, you carefully avoided overstepping by touching base with your coworker, and then you intervened even though it was uncomfortable. End by emphasizing antibias values and the majority's responsibility for addressing and fixing the problem.

In this way, you can help to create a new norm in your organization.[4] It matters that you do this during the peak of this social movement. But it is also essential to do this again in the following months, to show sustained support of antibias values.

Back Up Women and Racial Minorities

Minorities and women often want to confront biased comments, but they feel held back by the potential social and professional costs. Our research found that majority group members and men have a role to play in empowering women and racial minorities who want to speak up to verbally confront a biased comment.[5] The key is how you use your social network.

In six studies ($N = 2{,}163$), we compared women who were sought after for advice by others in their workplace (that is, those in *central* social network positions) to women who were not (that is, those in *peripheral* social network positions). We found that women in central advice network positions were statistically significantly more likely to confront gender bias. This was true both when women thought about how they *would* behave in a scenario that described a coworker making a biased comment to them, and when they reported how they *had* behaved when they had experienced bias in the workplace in the past. Even when the person who made the sexist comment in the scenario was the woman's boss, or when we reminded women of the risks of speaking out, being central in the advice network predicted women's confronting of gender bias. Why? An important factor was that women who are central in their advice networks believe their coworkers are similarly offended by gender bias and support their confronting it.

The key lesson for men and majority group members from our research is this: When you include individuals who are the targets of stereotyping and bias in your network, you and others signal to them that diversity and equitable treatment are important values. If you hear the comment, of course seize the moment to speak out. But even if you are not there to witness it, your inclusion of underrepresented colleagues in your network can empower them to speak out.

How do you purposefully transform your social network? Majority group members and men must begin practicing what we call an active inclusion approach.

Put Active Inclusion into Practice

Think about your social network. If you are a man or majority group member in your national context, it is almost certain that the people in your network are overwhelmingly demographically similar to you. Decades of research backs this up.[6] As a result, any individual who is in a numerical minority, such as racial minorities in leadership or women in STEM fields, are excluded from the informal life of their organizations or teams. This exclusion has negative consequences, not only for the careers of women and racial minorities, but also for their sense of belonging at work.

In our teaching and consulting, we find that majority group members are rarely aware that this is happening until we show them the data from their own organizations or networks. We have also come to understand that leaders almost never consider how the informal exclusion of women and racial minorities might be undermining their well-intentioned diversity and inclusion corporate initiatives.

Passive exclusion must be countered with active inclusion. That means that if you are a man or a majority group member, you must make an effort to bring women and racial minorities into your informal social network. Actively include your minority and women colleagues in informal meetings and discussions (whether they are focused on work or fun), seek their advice on issues relevant to their work expertise (not just their identities), and uncover commonalities as well as the ways you can learn from them. These interactions might be awkward or stressful at first, but they must not take on a paternalistic "I'm here to help you" tone.[7] You should ready yourself to learn some potentially unpleasant realities about the world as you might have failed to perceive it, about yourself, or about people you otherwise like and admire. Minorities and women constantly navigate a world in which they work to make the majority group members around them comfortable, which often means minimizing bias they experience in organizations.

An active inclusion approach to social networking requires you to forge a real relationship, one in which your minority and women colleagues can share both their professional expertise and their experience of the world with you, without having to anticipate backlash from you, or disappointment with your response, when they do. To achieve this, make sure you signal that you respect (in addition to like) these colleagues—it is critical that they know you see them as equals.[8]

Active inclusion goes beyond simply extending invitations. It also means using the power of your network connections in service of supporting your women and minority colleagues. Introduce women and racial minorities to people in your network who they would otherwise find difficult to meet. When an opportunity comes to you through your network (such as when you're asked to contribute to a special project at work or sit on a panel), offer the opportunity to a woman or racial minority instead, or offer yourself up as a package deal to present together. This doesn't mean giving them the less desirable opportunities; it means sharing opportunities that would be beneficial to your career.

This is the essence of antiracism and antisexism work: giving up your privilege to make things more equitable. And you can start with your social network.

Adapted from content posted on hbr.org, July 13, 2020 (product #H05Q6N).

NOTES

Chapter 2

1. Han Z. Li, "Cooperative and Intrusive Interruptions in Inter- and Intracultural Dyadic Discourse," *Journal of Language and Social Psychology* 20, no. 3 (September 2001), https://interruptions.net/literature/Li-JLSP01.pdf.

2. Kumiko Murata, "Intrusive or Co-operative? A Cross-Cultural Study of Interruption," *Journal of Pragmatics* 21, no. 4 (1994): 385–400, https://doi.org/10.1016/0378-2166(94)90011-6.

3. Lynn Smith-Lovin, "Interruptions in Group Discussions: The Effects of Gender and Group Composition," *American Sociological Review* 54 (1989).

4. Leigh Plunkett Tost, Francesca Gino, and Richard P. Larrick, "Power, Competitiveness, and Advice Taking: Why the Powerful Don't Listen," *Organizational Behavior and Human Decision Processes* 117, no. 1 (2012): 53–65, https://doi.org/10.1016/j.obhdp.2011.10.001.

5. Leigh Plunkett Tost, Francesca Gino, and Richard P. Larrick, "When Power Makes Others Speechless: The Negative Impact of Leader Power on Team Performance," *Academy of Management Journal* 56, no. 5 (2012), https://doi.org/10.5465/amj.2011.0180.

Chapter 5

1. Ksenia Keplinger et al., "Women at Work: Changes in Sexual Harassment Between September 2016 and September 2018," *PLoS ONE* 14, no. 7 (2019): e0218313, https://doi.org/10.1371/journal.pone.0218313.

2. L. F. Fitzgerald and L. M. Cortina, "Sexual Harassment in Work Organizations: A View from the 21st Century," in *APA Handbook of the Psychology of Women: Perspectives on Women's Private and Public Lives*, eds. C. B. Travis et al. (American Psychological Association, 2018), 215–234, https://doi.org/10.1037/0000060-012.

3. Nathan Heller, "The Gig Economy Is Especially Susceptible to Sexual Harassment," *New Yorker*, January 25, 2018, https://www.newyorker.com/culture/cultural-comment/the-gig-economy-is-especially-susceptible-to-sexual-harassment.

Chapter 6

1. M. L. Fransen, E. G. Smit, and P. W. Verlegh, "Strategies and Motives for Resistance to Persuasion: An Integrative Framework," *Frontiers in Psychology* 6 (2015): 1201, doi:10.3389/fpsyg.2015.01201.

Chapter 7

1. Nikki Graf, "Sexual Harassment at Work in the Era of #MeToo," Pew Research Center Social & Demographic Trends, April 4, 2018, https://www.pewresearch.org/social-trends/2018/04/04/sexual-harassment-at-work-in-the-era-of-metoo/; R. Ilies et al., "Reported Incidence Rates of Work-Related Sexual Harassment in the United States: Using Meta-Analysis to Explain Reported Rate Disparities," *Personnel Psychology* 56 (2003): 607–631, https://doi.org/10.1111/j.1744-6570.2003.tb00752.x.

2. Frank Dobbin and Alexandra Kalev, "The Promise and Peril of Sexual Harassment Programs," *Proceedings of the National Academy of Sciences* 116, no. 25 (June 2019): 12255–12260, doi: 10.1073/pnas.1818477116.

3. S. G. Bingham and L. L. Scherer, "The Unexpected Effects of a Sexual Harassment Educational Program," *Journal of Applied Behavioral Science* 37, no. 2 (2001): 125–153, doi:10.1177/0021886301372001.

4. L. A. Robb and D. Doverspike, "Self-Reported Proclivity to Harass as a Moderator of the Effectiveness of Sexual

Harassment-Prevention Training," *Psychological Reports* 88, no. 1 (2001): 85–88, doi:10.2466/pr0.2001.88.1.85.

5. K. A. Lonsway, L. M. Cortina, and V. J. Magley, "Sexual Harassment Mythology: Definition, Conceptualization, and Measurement," *Sex Roles* 58 (2008): 599–615, https://doi.org/10.1007/s11199-007-9367-1.

6. H. McLaughlin, C. Uggen, and A. Blackstone, "The Economic and Career Effects of Sexual Harassment on Working Women," *Gender and Society* 31 (2017): 333–358.

7. M. E. Bergman et al., "The (Un)reasonableness of Reporting: Antecedents and Consequences of Reporting Sexual Harassment," *Journal of Applied Psychology* 87, no. 2 (2002): 230–242, doi: 10.1037/0021-9010.87.2.230.

8. J. Tinkler, S. Gremillion, and K. Arthurs, "Legal Messengers, Gender, and Sexual Harassment Policy Training," *Law & Social Inquiry* 40 (2015): 152–174, https://doi.org/10.1111/lsi.12065.

Chapter 8

1. Insiya Hussain et al., "The Voice Bystander Effect: How Information Redundancy Inhibits Employee Voice," *Academy of Management Journal* 62 (2019): 828–849, https://doi.org/10.5465/amj.2017.0245.

2. Ethan R. Burris, "The Risks and Rewards of Speaking Up: Managerial Responses to Employee Voice," *Academy of Management Journal* 55 (2012): 851–875, https://doi.org/10.5465/amj.2010.0562.

Chapter 10

1. Center for Talent Innovation, "What #MeToo Means for Corporate America," July 11, 2018, https://www.talentinnovation.org/Research-and-Insights/pop_page.cfm?publication=1620.

2. Olga Khazan, "Why Men Sexually Harass Women," *Atlantic*, October 5, 2018, https://www.theatlantic.com/science/archive/2018/10/why-do-more-men-women-sexually-harass/572221/.

3. J. R. Thorpe, "No, Woman-on-Woman Sexual Harassment Is Not a Myth," *Bustle,* March 31, 2017, https://www.bustle.com/p/no-woman-on-woman-sexual-harassment-is-not-a-myth-46130.

4. Audrea Lim, "The Alt-Right's Asian Fetish," *New York Times,* January 6, 2018, https://www.nytimes.com/2018/01/06/opinion/sunday/alt-right-asian-fetish.html?login=smartlock&auth=login-smartlock.

5. Farai Chideya with Herbert Samuels, "Sex Stereotypes of African Americans Have Long History," NPR, May 7, 2007, https://www.npr.org/templates/story/story.php?storyId=10057104; Wesley Morris, "Last Taboo: Why Pop Culture Just Can't Deal with Black Male Sexuality," *New York Times,* October 27, 2016, https://www.nytimes.com/interactive/2016/10/30/magazine/black-male-sexuality-last-taboo.html.

6. Julie Creswell, Kevin Draper, and Rachel Abrams, "At Nike, Revolt Led by Women Leads to Exodus of Male Executives," *New York Times,* April 28, 2018, https://www.nytimes.com/2018/04/28/business/nike-women.html.

Chapter 11

1. T. D. Maynes and P. M. Podsakoff, "Speaking More Broadly: An Examination of the Nature, Antecedents, and Consequences of an Expanded Set of Employee Voice Behaviors," *Journal of Applied Psychology* 99, no. 1 (2014): 87–112, doi: 10.1037/a0034284; J. R. Detert et al., "Voice Flows to and Around Leaders: Understanding When Units Are Helped or Hurt by Employee Voice," *Administrative Science Quarterly* 58, no. 4 (2013): 624–668, doi:10.1177/0001839213510151.

2. J. R. Detert and E. A. Bruno, "Workplace Courage: Review, Synthesis, and Future Agenda for a Complex Construct," *Academy of Management Annals* 11, no. 2 (2017): 593–639, https://doi.org/10.5465/annals.2015.0155.

3. Adia Harvey Wingfield, "Are Some Emotions Marked 'Whites Only'? Racialized Feeling Rules in Professional Workplaces," *Social Problems* 57, no. 2 (2010): 251–268, https://doi.org/10.1525/sp.2010.57.2.251.

4. Jane E. Dutton, Laura Morgan Roberts, and Jeffrey Bednar, "Pathways for Positive Identity Construction at Work: Four Types of Positive Identity and the Building of Social Resources," *Academy of Management Review* 35, no. 2 (2017): 265–293, https://doi.org/10.5465/amr.35.2.zok265.

5. Laura Morgan Roberts, "Move Beyond the Business Case for Diversity," *Bloomberg*, June 28, 2020, https://www.bloomberg.com/opinion/articles/2020-06-28/business-case-for-diversity-isn-t-enough-to-end-corporate-racism.

Chapter 12

1. D. W. Sue et al., "Racial Microaggressions in Everyday Life: Implications for Clinical Practice," *American Psychologist* 62, no. 4 (2007): 271–286, doi: 10.1037/0003-066X.62.4.271.

2. K. P. Jones et al., "Not So Subtle: A Meta-Analytic Investigation of the Correlates of Subtle and Overt Discrimination," *Journal of Management* 42, no. 6 (2016): 1588–1613, doi:10.1177/0149206313506466.

3. Dnika J. Travis, Jennifer Thorpe-Moscon, and Courtney McCluney, "Emotional Tax: How Black Women and Men Pay More at Work and How Leaders Can Take Action," Catalyst, January 2019, https://www.catalyst.org/wp-content/uploads/2019/01/emotional_tax_how_black_women_and_men_pay_more.pdf.

4. R. W. Livingston, A. S. Rosette, and E. F. Washington, "Can an Agentic Black Woman Get Ahead? The Impact of Race and Interpersonal Dominance on Perceptions of Female Leaders," *Psychological Science* 23, no. 4 (2012): 354–358, doi:10.1177/0956797611428079.

5. Siobhan Neela-Stock, "How to Recognize If You're Being Racially Gaslighted," *Mashable*, June 26, 2020, https://mashable.com/article/how-to-recognize-racial-gaslighting/; Natalie Morris, "What Is 'Racial Gaslighting'—and Why Is It So Damaging for People of Colour?," *Metro*, June 18, 2020, https://metro.co.uk/2020/06/18/what-racial-gaslighting-why-damaging-people-colour-12866409/.

6. M. Afzalur Rahim, "A Measure of Styles of Handling Interpersonal Conflict," *Academy of Management Journal* 26, no. 2 (1983): 368–376, doi:10.2307/255985.

7. Sam Louie, "Working While Black," *Psychology Today,* April 6, 2017, https://www.psychologytoday.com/us/blog/minority-report/201704/working-while-black.

8. D. W. Sue, "Race Talk: The Psychology of Racial Dialogues," *American Psychologist* 68, no. 8 (2013): 663–672, https://doi.org/10.1037/a0033681.

9. Kristen Rogers, "Dear Anti-Racist Allies: Here's How to Respond to Microaggressions," CNN, June 6, 2020, https://www.cnn.com/2020/06/05/health/racial-microaggressions-examples-responses-wellness/index.html.

10. Erika V. Hall et al., "MOSAIC: A Model of Stereotyping Through Associated and Intersectional Categories," *Academy of Management Review* 44, no. 3 (2019): 643–672, https://doi.org/10.5465/amr.2017.0109.

11. Courtney Lynn McCluney et al., "Calling in Black: Dynamic Model of Racially Traumatic Events on Organizational Resourcing," *Academy of Management Proceedings*, 2017, https://doi.org/10.5465/AMBPP.2017.301.

12. Delonte Gholston, "When Joy Is an Act of Resistance," *Huffpost*, June 23, 2017, https://www.huffpost.com/entry/joy-is-an-act-of-resistance_b_594cb975e4b0c85b96c6584b.

Chapter 13

1. AACSB, *Business School Data Guide 2020*, https://www.aacsb.edu/-/media/aacsb/publications/data-trends-booklet/2020.ashx?la=en&hash=DD37BBF79457F638BBB43C19A72F1840121796D6.

2. National Center for Education Studies, "Characteristics of Postsecondary Faculty," *The Condition of Education 2020*, May 2020, https://nces.ed.gov/programs/coe/indicator/csc.

3. Elizabeth Umphress et al., "When Birds of a Feather Flock Together and When They Do Not: Status Composition, Social

Dominance Orientation, and Organizational Attractiveness," *Journal of Applied Psychology* 92 (2007): 396–409.

4. Julianna Pillemer, Elizabeth R. Graham, and Deborah M. Burke, "The Face Says It All: CEOs, Gender, and Predicting Corporate Performance," *Leadership Quarterly* 25, no. 5 (2014): 855–864, https://doi.org/10.1016/j.leaqua.2014.07.002.

5. Susan Bartel, "Leadership Barriers for Women in Higher Education," *BizEd*, December 19, 2018, https://bized.aacsb.edu/articles/2018/12/leadership-barriers-for-women-in-higher-education.

Chapter 14

1. Joan C. Williams and Marina Multhaup, "For Women and Minorities to Get Ahead, Managers Must Assign Work Fairly," hbr.org, March 5, 2018, https://hbr.org/2018/03/for-women-and-minorities-to-get-ahead-managers-must-assign-work-fairly.

2. J. Berdahl and C. Moore, "Workplace Harassment: Double Jeopardy for Minority Women," *Journal of Applied Psychology* 91, no. 2 (2006): 426–436.

3. M. E. Heilman and J. J. Chen, "Same Behavior, Different Consequences: Reactions to Men's and Women's Altruistic Citizenship Behavior," *Journal of Applied Psychology* 90, no. 3 (2005): 431–441, https://doi.org/10.1037/0021-9010.90.3.431.

4. Ekaterina Netchaeva, Maryam Kouchaki, and Leah D. Sheppard, "A Man's (Precarious) Place: Men's Experienced Threat and Self-Assertive Reactions to Female Superiors," *Personality and Social Psychology Bulletin* 41, no. 9 (September 2015): 1247–1259, https://doi.org/10.1177/0146167215593491.

5. D. L. Kidder, "The Influence of Gender on the Performance of Organizational Citizenship Behaviors," *Journal of Management* 28, no. 5 (2002): 629–648, https://doi.org/10.1177/014920630202800504.

6. Ruchika Tulshyan, "The 'I Just Can't Say No' Club Women Need to Advance in Their Careers," *Forbes*, June 28, 2016, https://www.forbes.com/sites/ruchikatulshyan/2016/06/28/the-i-just-cant-say-no-club-women-need-to-advance-in-their-careers/?sh=111ebef84917.

Chapter 15

1. "Majority of Men Support Gender Equality—Ipsos Global Study," Ipsos, March 6, 2019, https://www.ipsos.com/en-au/majority-men-support-gender-equality-ipsos-global-study.

2. "So, You Want to Be a Male Ally for Gender Equality? (And You Should): Results from a National Survey, and a Few Things You Should Know," Promundo, n.d., https://promundoglobal.org/resources/male-allyship/.

3. S. J. Gervais and A. L. Hillard, "Confronting Sexism as Persuasion: Effects of a Confrontation's Recipient, Source, Message, and Context," *Journal of Social Issues* 70, no. 4 (2014): 653–667, https://doi.org/10.1111/josi.12084.

4. Heather M. Rasinski and Alexander M. Czopp, "The Effect of Target Status on Witnesses' Reactions to Confrontations of Bias," *Basic and Applied Social Psychology* 32, no. 1 (2010): 8–16, doi: 10.1080/01973530903539754.

5. F. Mols et al., "Why a Nudge Is Not Enough," *European Journal of Political Research* 54, no. 1 (2015): 81–98, https://doi.org/10.1111/1475-6765.12073.

6. C. Kilmartin et al., "A Behavior Intervention to Reduce Sexism in College Men," *Gender Issues* 32 (2015): 97–110, https://doi.org/10.1007/s12147-014-9130-1.

Chapter 16

1. "The Study on White Men: Leading Diversity Through Inclusion," Greatheart Leader Labs, January 2013, http://www.whitemensleadershipstudy.com/pdf/WMLS%20Executive%20Summary.pdf.

2. Elliot Aronson and Shelley Patnoe, *The Jigsaw Classroom: Building Cooperation in the Classroom*, 2nd ed. (London: Longman, 1997).

Chapter 17

1. N. A. Christakis and J. H. Fowler, "Social Contagion Theory: Examining Dynamic Social Networks and Human Behavior,"

Statistics in Medicine 32, no. 4 (2013): 556–577, https://doi.org/10.1002/sim.5408.

2. N. A. Christakis and J. H. Fowler, "The Spread of Obesity in a Large Social Network over 32 Years," *New England Journal of Medicine* 357, no. 4 (2007): 370–379, doi: 10.1056/NEJMsa066082; Herminia Ibarra and Steven B. Andrews, "Power, Social Influence, and Sense Making: Effects of Network Centrality and Proximity on Employee Perceptions," *Administrative Science Quarterly* 38, no. 2 (1993): 277–303, doi:10.2307/2393414; Rose McDermott, James H. Fowler, and Nicholas A. Christakis, "Breaking Up Is Hard to Do, Unless Everyone Else Is Doing It Too: Social Network Effects on Divorce in a Longitudinal Sample," *Social Forces* 92, no. 2 (2013): 491–519, https://doi.org/10.1093/sf/sot096.

3. R. I. M. Dunbar and Susanne Shultz, "Evolution in the Social Brain," *Science*, September 7, 2007, 1344–1347, https://science.sciencemag.org/content/317/5843/1344/tab-article-info.

4. F. A. Blanchard et al., "Condemning and Condoning Racism: A Social Context Approach to Interracial Settings," *Journal of Applied Psychology* 79, no. 6 (1994): 993–997, https://doi.org/10.1037/0021-9010.79.6.993.

5. Raina A. Brands and Aneeta Rattan, "Perceived Centrality in Social Networks Increases Women's Expectations of Confronting Sexism," *Personality and Social Psychology Bulletin* 46, no. 12 (December 2020): 1682–1701, https://doi.org/10.1177/0146167220912621.

6. Raina Brands and Anna Johnston, "I Like You: You're Like Me," *Think at London Business School*, March 3, 2020, https://www.london.edu/think/i-like-you-youre-like-me.

7. Jennifer A. Richeson and J. Nicole Shelton, "Negotiating Interracial Interactions: Costs, Consequences, and Possibilities," *Current Directions in Psychological Science* 16, no. 6 (December 2007): 316–320, https://doi.org/10.1111/j.1467-8721.2007.00528.x; D. R. Avery et al., "It Does Not Have to Be Uncomfortable: The Role of Behavioral Scripts in Black–White Interracial Interactions," *Journal of Applied Psychology* 94, no. 6 (2009): 1382–1393, https://doi.org/10.1037/a0016208; Sophie Trawalter and Jennifer A. Richeson, "Let's Talk About Race, Baby! When Whites' and Blacks' Interracial Contact Experiences Diverge," *Journal of Experimental Social*

Psychology 44, no. 4 (2008): 1214–1217, https://doi.org/10.1016/j.jesp.2008.03.013.

8. H. B. Bergsieker, J. N. Shelton, and J. A. Richeson, "To Be Liked Versus Respected: Divergent Goals in Interracial Interactions," *Journal of Personality and Social Psychology* 99, no. 2 (2010), 248–264, https://doi.org/10.1037/a0018474.

INDEX

Index

Discussion Guide

Since the *Women at Work* podcast first launched, we've heard from all over the world that it has inspired discussions and listening groups. We hope that this book does the same—that you'll want to share what you've learned with others. The questions in this discussion guide will help you talk about the challenges women face in the workplace and how we can work together to overcome them.

You don't need to have read the book from start to finish to participate. To get the most out of your discussion, think about the size of your group. A big group has the advantage of spreading ideas more widely—whether throughout your organization or among your friends and peers—but might lose some of the honesty and connection a small group would have. You may want to assign someone to lead the discussion to ensure that all participants are included, especially if some attendees are joining virtually. And it's a good idea to establish ground rules around privacy and confidentiality. *Women at Work* topics touch on difficult issues surrounding sexism and racism, so consider using trigger warnings.

Finally, think about what you want to accomplish in your discussion. Do you want to create a network of mutual support? Hope to disrupt the status quo? Or are you simply looking for an empathetic ear? With your goals in mind, use the questions that follow to advance the conversation about women at work.

1. When you spoke out on a big issue in the past, how did you prepare? Did you speak up in the moment, without preparation, while the incident and its impact was fresh in your mind? Or did you take steps to prepare before you spoke, such as writing down the points you wanted to make? Did you pace and rehearse aloud alone what you planned to say? Did you partner with a friend or trusted colleague? What did you learn about preparing for an effective outcome? Would you do anything differently now?

2. Do you know your company's antidiscrimination and sexual harassment policies? If not, do you know where to find them? If you know them, do you think they are effective? Has your company updated any of its policies in response to the movements of the past few years? What recommendations would you give to shore up areas where you think they are lacking?

3. In chapter 4, Amy Gallo says that she was hopeful there would be some change based on #MeToo and asked Marianne Cooper, "Did you expect to see a difference?" How would you answer this question? Has your perspective changed in the years since the #MeToo movement in 2018?

4. In the "Women in the Workplace 2018" report, approximately 50% of women surveyed said that reporting harassment would lead to a fair and effective investigation, versus approximately 70% of men. How confident are you in your company's ability to fairly and effectively manage reports of sexual harassment? Why do you feel this way?

5. What's one thing you would suggest to your leadership team to improve the climate for women and people of color in your organization? How can you create a culture of collective accountability?

6. With the story she shares in chapter 9, Sarah Beaulieu acknowledges that speaking out is physically and emotionally uncomfortable even for her (and it's her life's work). How can you encourage yourself and others to lean into the discomfort and learn?

7. What are you likely to do the next time you experience or witness microaggression or harassment in your workplace? If you're unlikely to speak out, why not? What conditions would need to be in place for you to feel more comfortable speaking up? How has your thinking about this evolved?

8. What experience do you have with being asked to do office housework? How have you handled it in the past? Have the requests changed as you've advanced

in your career? How would you like to try fielding these demands after reading this book and participating in this discussion group?

9. Can you think of instances where you demonstrated some of the gendered tendencies that Deborah Tannen outlines in chapter 1? How did your counterpart respond? Can you think of ways to interrupt these patterns?

10. Do you often use "we" when talking about something you accomplished? Over the next few weeks, notice when you say "we" instead of "I" and think about how you can give yourself more credit.

11. Have you ever talked to an overtalker or interrupter to address the issue head-on? If not, is this something you can see yourself doing? Have you witnessed any colleagues manage this effectively?

12. What do you do to take care of yourself after having a difficult conversation?

13. After reading this book and participating in this discussion group, name one step you'll take to create a more welcoming and safe culture:

    - **Short term:** tomorrow
    - **Longer term:** this month
    - **Longest term:** this fiscal year

ABOUT THE CONTRIBUTORS

Amy Bernstein, *Women at Work* cohost, is the editor of *Harvard Business Review* and vice president and executive editorial director of Harvard Business Publishing. Follow her on Twitter @asbernstein2185.

Sarah Green Carmichael, *Women at Work* cohost (seasons 1–2), is an editor and columnist at Bloomberg Opinion and a former executive editor at *Harvard Business Review.* Follow her on Twitter @skgreen.

Amy Gallo, *Women at Work* cohost, is a contributing editor at *Harvard Business Review* and the author of the *HBR Guide to Dealing with Conflict* (Harvard Business Review Press, 2017) and *Getting Along: How to Work with Anyone (Even Difficult People)* (Harvard Business Review Press, 2022). She writes and speaks about workplace dynamics. Watch her TEDx talk on conflict and follow her on Twitter @amyegallo.

Amanda Kersey, *Women at Work* producer, is a senior audio producer at *Harvard Business Review.*

Nicole Torres, *Women at Work* cohost (seasons 1–4), is an editor at Bloomberg Opinion based in London and a former senior editor at *Harvard Business Review.*

Liza Barnes is a doctoral candidate in organizational behavior at Leeds School of Business, University of Colorado Boulder. Her research interests sit at the intersection of identity management, organizational compassion, and positive relationships at work.

Sarah Pierson Beaulieu is the author of *Breaking the Silence Habit: A Practical Guide to Uncomfortable Conversations in the #MeToo Workplace.*

Alison Hall Birch is an assistant professor at the College of Business at the University of Texas, Arlington, where she studies stigma-based bias, diversity management, and leadership.

Trudy Bourgeois is the founder of the Center for Workforce Excellence and is a renowned and respected authority on leadership development, diversity, equity, and inclusion. She is the author of *Her Corner Office, The Hybrid Leader,* and *Equality: Courageous Conversations About Women, Men, and Race in the Workplace to Create* *a Diversity and Inclusion Breakthrough* and coauthor of *Business Success Secrets.*

Raina Brands is an associate professor at University College London School of Management and a cofounder of Career Equally. She is an expert in social networks and how these informal workplace relationships can present hidden barriers to performance, attainment, and collaboration. A core focus of her research is to understand how social networks shape women's careers and to directly intervene in these processes to create more meritocratic organizations.

Lan Nguyen Chaplin is an associate professor of marketing at the University of Illinois at Chicago. She is also the founder of QuanTâm, a nonprofit that gives young professionals opportunities to expand their networks and sharpen their professional skills while serving their communities.

Marianne Cooper is a senior research scholar at the VMware Women's Leadership Innovation Lab at Stanford University.

James R. Detert is the author of *Choosing Courage* (Harvard Business Review Press, 2021) and the John L. Colley Professor of Business Administration at the University of Virginia's Darden School of Business.

Frank Dobbin is the Henry Ford II Professor and Chair of the Department of Sociology at Harvard University.

Francesca Gino is a behavioral scientist and the Tandon Family Professor of Business Administration at Harvard Business School. She is the author of the books *Rebel Talent: Why It Pays to Break the Rules at Work and in Life* and *Sidetracked: Why Our Decisions Get Derailed, and How We Can Stick to the Plan*. Follow her on Twitter @francescagino.

Insiya Hussain is an assistant professor of management at the University of Texas at Austin McCombs School of Business. Her research is focused on understanding how employees can overcome the challenges they face when trying to speak up with their ideas, advocate social issues, and negotiate for personal rewards. Follow her on Twitter @Insiya_H.

Pooja Jain-Link is executive vice president at Coqual, where she coleads the organization's research and advisory services practices that examine workplace culture and the systemic change needed to create equity. She's led research for many Coqual studies, including *Being Black in Corporate America*, *The Sponsor Dividend*, and *Wonder Women in STEM and Companies That Champion Them*.

Stefanie K. Johnson is an associate professor of management and entrepreneurship at the University of Colorado's

Leeds School of Business and author of *Inclusify*. Johnson studies the intersection of leadership and diversity, focusing on how unconscious bias affects the evaluation of leaders, and strategies that leaders can use to mitigate bias. She is a member of Marshall Goldsmith 100 Coaches and the 2020 Thinkers50 Radar List.

W. Brad Johnson is a professor of psychology in the Department of Leadership, Ethics, and Law at the United States Naval Academy and a faculty associate in the Graduate School of Education at Johns Hopkins University. He is the coauthor of *Good Guys: How Men Can Be Better Allies for Women in the Workplace*, *Athena Rising: How and Why Men Should Mentor Women*, *The Elements of Mentoring*, and other books on mentorship.

Alexandra Kalev is an associate professor of sociology and anthropology at Tel Aviv University.

Julia Taylor Kennedy is executive vice president at Coqual, where she coleads the organization's research and leadership development practices to support diverse, inclusive, and equitable leadership in the workplace. She's led research for many Coqual studies, including *Being Black in Corporate America*, *The Power of Belonging*, and *The Sponsor Dividend*.

Ksenia Keplinger leads the independent research group Organizational Leadership and Diversity at the Max

Planck Institute for Intelligent Systems in Stuttgart, Germany. She studies the intersection of leadership, diversity, and artificial intelligence, focusing on ways to mitigate bias in human-machine interaction and the nature of leadership in the AI age.

Jessica F. Kirk is an assistant professor of management at the Fogelman College of Business and Economics at the University of Memphis. She studies how stereotyping leads to mistreatment and biased perceptions of women and minorities and has partnered with government institutions, technology accelerators, and *Fortune* 500 corporations in order to explore these dynamics in a variety of contexts.

Aneeta Rattan is an associate professor of organizational behavior at London Business School and a cofounder of Career Equally. Her research focuses on using mindsets and diversity messages to foster an equal sense of belonging among underrepresented groups and to effectively confront stereotyping, prejudice, and inequity in the workplace.

Kathleen Kelley Reardon is professor emerita at the University of Southern California Marshall School of Business and an expert in workplace politics, persuasion, and negotiation. She is the author of Amazon bestsellers *The Secret Handshake*, *It's All Politics*, and *Comebacks at Work*.

Laura Morgan Roberts is a professor of practice at the University of Virginia's Darden School of Business and the coeditor of *Race, Work, and Leadership: New Perspectives on the Black Experience* (Harvard Business Review Press, 2019).

David G. Smith is an associate professor in the Johns Hopkins Carey Business School. He is the coauthor, with W. Brad Johnson, of *Good Guys: How Men Can Be Better Allies for Women in the Workplace* and *Athena Rising: How and Why Men Should Mentor Women.*

Amy Jen Su is a cofounder and managing partner of Paravis Partners, a premier executive coaching and leadership development firm. For the past two decades, she has coached CEOs, executives, and rising stars in organizations. She is the author of *The Leader You Want to Be: Five Essential Principles for Bringing Out Your Best Self—Every Day* (Harvard Business Review Press, 2019) and a coauthor, with Muriel Maignan Wilkins, of *Own the Room: Discover Your Signature Voice to Master Your Leadership Presence* (Harvard Business Review Press, 2013).

Subra Tangirala is Dean's Professor of Management and Organization at Robert H. Smith School of Business, University of Maryland. In his research, he explores why employees might fail to speak up when they have concerns, opinions, or ideas to share, and the consequences to organizations when employees remain silent.

Deborah Tannen is a university professor and professor of linguistics at Georgetown University and the author of many books, including *Talking from 9 to 5: Women and Men at Work*, the bestseller *You Just Don't Understand: Women and Men in Conversation*, and most recently, *Finding My Father: His Century-Long Journey from World War I Warsaw and My Quest to Follow.*

Ruchika Tulshyan is the founder of Candour, an inclusion strategy firm. She writes regularly for the *New York Times* and *Harvard Business Review* on workplace inclusion. Her latest book is *Inclusion on Purpose: An Intersectional Approach to Creating a Culture of Belonging at Work.*

Ella F. Washington is a professor of practice at Georgetown University's McDonough School of Business and the founder of Ellavate Solutions, which provides diversity and inclusion strategy and training for organizations. She cohosts the weekly podcast *Cultural Competence.*

Lily Zheng is a diversity, equity, and inclusion strategist and executive coach who works with organizations to create high-impact and sustainable change. They are the coauthor of *Gender Ambiguity in the Workplace: Transgender and Gender-Diverse Discrimination* and *The Ethical Sellout: Maintaining Your Integrity in the Age of Compromise.*

Women *at* Work

Inspiring conversations, advancing together

ABOUT THE PODCAST

Women face gender discrimination throughout our careers. It doesn't have to derail our ambitions—but how do we prepare to deal with it? There's no workplace orientation session about narrowing the wage gap, standing up to interrupting male colleagues, or taking on many other issues we encounter at work. So HBR staffers Amy Bernstein, Amy Gallo, and Emily Caulfield are untangling some of the knottiest problems. They interview experts on gender, tell stories about their own experiences, and give lots of practical advice to help you succeed in spite of the obstacles.

Listen and subscribe:

Apple Podcasts, Google Podcasts, Spotify, RSS